☀️ INSIGHT P

COSTA DEL SUL

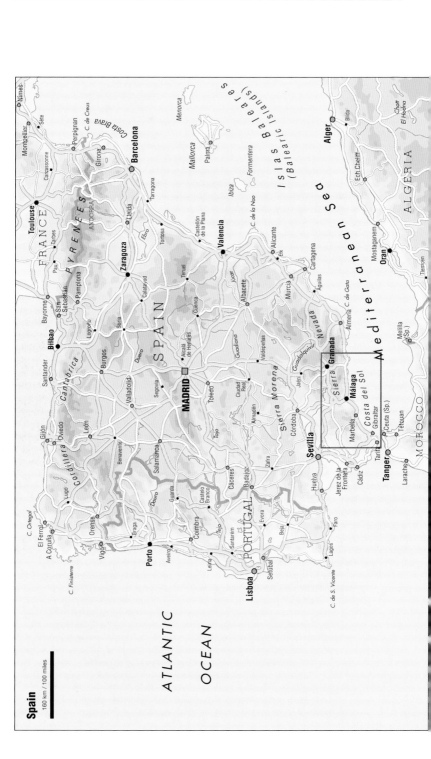

Spain
160 km / 100 miles

Welcome

This is one of 133 itinerary-based *Pocket Guides* produced by the editors of Insight Guides, whose books have set the standard for visual travel guides since 1970. With top-quality photography and authoritative recommendations, this guidebook aims to help visitors get the most out of this beautiful region during a short stay. With this in mind, Insight Guides' correspondent on the Costa del Sol, Barnard Collings, has devised a range of itineraries, combining lazy days on the beach with drives through some of Spain's loveliest scenery.

Using Marbella as a springboard (though any of the other resorts will serve as well), he has devised 19 itineraries, ranging from walking tours of the main resorts and short drives along the coast to longer excursions to major attractions inland, such as the spectacularly sited town of Ronda, elegant Antequera and the famous 'white towns'. Supporting the tours are chapters on history and culture, shopping, eating out and nightlife, plus a calendar of events and practical information, which includes detailed hotel listings.

Barnard Collings is a long-time resident of Marbella. He first visited the region with friends when he was in his mid-twenties. While his companions threw themselves into infiltrating Marbella's high society, he set off to explore quiet inland villages. Today, Collings is as fond as anyone of the pleasures the Costa offers, especially its many excellent restaurants, but he retains his passion for plunging off the beaten track to discover the quintessential Spain.

For the 2001 edition, the late Mark Little, a regular Insight contributor for many years, who lived in the pretty Costa town of Mijas, provided new listings sections and added the new excursions to Cádiz and Gibraltar. The 2002, 2004 and 2007 editions were updated by Josephine Quintero, Siân Lezard and Nick Inman, respectively.

HISTORY AND CULTURE

An introduction to the Costa del Sol's eventful history and rich culture, from the rise of Moorish Andalucía to the region's rebirth as a leading holiday destination.....**11**

ITINERARIES

The first three tours explore Marbella, Málaga and surroundings; tours 4–8 visit picturesque inland villages; routes 9–13 offer a variety of excursions and activities; and tours 14–19 explore further afield, to Tarifa, Cádiz, Gibraltar and the Costa Tropical.

1   **Discovering Marbella** is a tour of the town's shady streets, bright white houses and pretty squares. Round off the tour with a walk down the Avenida del Mar..........**22**

2   **A Drive around Marbella** takes you to Puerto Banús, playground of the rich, and into the hills for lunch in the pretty village of Benhavís.................................**25**

3   **Málaga** explores this historic city taking in the Cathedral, the Picasso Museum, the Moorish Alcazaba, and the Castillo de Gibralfaro **28**

4   **Ronda** is a scenic drive through the mountains to one of Spain's most beautiful towns. Spectacular natural sights include the Tajo (gorge), while man-made creations encompass palaces, churches, museums, the ruins of Arab baths and one of Spain's oldest bullrings **32**

5   **Ronda By Rail** is a scenic journey through the hills, stopping at some pretty stations en route **36**

6   **Antequera** takes you to this historic town and its environs, whose many attractions range from prehistoric cave tombs to churches, Moorish remains and the Parque Natural El Torcal de Antequera **38**

7   **A Half-day in Istán** is an easy drive to a 9th-century mountain village **42**

8   **Lunch at the Refugio de Juanar** is a short trip into the hills behind Marbella for lunch at this popular hunting lodge. Afterwards a walk along the forested trails of the Sierra Blanca...**43**

9   **A Morning in Estepona** investigates Marbella's coastal neighbour, Estepona, and then takes a leisurely drive into the forest trails of the Sierra Bermeja **44**

10   **A Half-day in Casares** is a lovely drive to one of the Costa's least-spoilt *pueblos* **45**

11   **Gaucín, Castellar and Sotogrande** travels to the Moorish castles of Gaucín and Jimena de la Frontera ...**46**

12 **Ardales, Lakes and El Chorro** is a day's drive taking in *pueblos*, forts, lakes and El Chorro gorge **48**

13 **Mijas, Benalmádena and Torremolinos** explores the traditional village of Mijas, visits a Buddhist monument then takes in some children's entertainment before ending in the busy resort of Torremolinos **51**

14 **A Day in Gibraltar** samples the Rock's mixture of English and Spanish culture and visits the Apes' Den....**54**

15 **Tarifa, Windsurfing Capital** heads for the sandy shores of Spain's southern tip, visits Roman ruins at Baelo Claudia, a nudist beach and a former monastery.........**56**

16 **Mountain Villages** explores the pretty landscapes that surround Ronda, especially the villages of Grazalema and El Bosque and their popular hiking routes...........**59**

17 **Cádiz and Sherry Country** offers a taste of the fine wines of Jerez and the fresh shellfish of El Puerto de Santa María before visiting the ancient city of Cádiz **62**

18 **La Axarquía region, Nerja and Frigiliana** explores the coast and caves east of Marbella and Málaga........**64**

19 **The Costa Tropical** takes you east to the perfect bay of La Herradura, the Phoenician-founded village of Almuñecar and picturesque Salobreña............................**66**

LEISURE ACTIVITIES
What to buy, where to eat, and where to go **69–78**

CALENDAR OF EVENTS
A month by month list of all the main festivals...........**79**

PRACTICAL INFORMATION
All the background information you are likely to need for your stay, with a list of hand-picked hotels...........**81–89**

MAPS

Spain **4**		*Antequera*....................**38**	
The Costa del Sol ...**18–19**		*Western Costa del Sol* ..**43**	
Discovering Marbella ..**24**		*Eastern Costa del Sol* ..**50**	
Málaga **28**		*Gibraltar*......................**54**	
Ronda **33**		*Further West* **58**	

CREDITS AND INDEX
pages **91–96**

Pages 2–3: a taste of the good life on the Costa
Pages 8–9: a *pueble blanco* (white town) of the region

History &Culture

As a travel destination, the Costa del Sol offers the best of two worlds. It is one of Europe's top leisure resorts, with modern hotels, a wide variety of gourmet restaurants, plus beaches, casinos, yacht harbours, tennis clubs and the continent's largest concentration of golf courses. Add to that a wonderfully relaxed and cosmopolitan atmosphere. On the other hand, international character notwithstanding, this is Andalucía, Spain at its most picturesque and romantic. Venture a few miles inland and you come face to face with dramatic countryside and astounding cultural treasures.

Much has changed in southern Spain, and some may lament the loss of old traditions and values in modern-day Andalucía. Others are aghast at the frenzied urban development that, in a few decades, has transformed the whole coast between Málaga and Estepona into a vast conurbation of hotels, villa developments, golf courses and marinas. But most Andalusians don't regret the disappearance from their streets of donkeys and little old ladies wearing the perpetual black of mourning. Tourism has brought prosperity and a degree of modern comfort to a land long cursed by poverty and neglect. One thing that hasn't changed is the character of the Andalusians – open and tolerant towards visitors – a character shaped by 3,000 years of history.

Cave paintings dating from 20,000–15,000BC show that Palaeolithic man flourished in southern Iberia. Skeletons, artefacts and sanctuary sites located along the coast and inland are evidence of an important prehistoric culture here. Early civilisation flourished some 4,500 years ago around Antequera, where a people about whom little is known transported enormous stone slabs, some weighing up to 180 tons, across great distances and then moved them into position to construct dolmens (cave tombs).

Greeks Bearing Gifts

The mineral wealth of the various Andalusian mountain ranges attracted sea-faring visitors. First Phoenician traders from the Middle East established settlements at Malaka (Málaga) and Cádiz in around 1,000BC. Shortly afterwards Phoecean Greeks set up trading posts along the coastline. It was probably the Greeks who introduced the grape vines and olive trees that are such an essential part of the Andalusian landscape and culture today.

After the Phoenician and Greek influences waned in the Mediterranean, Carthage, the Phoenician offshoot state (in present-day Tunisia), took their place. But unlike their predecessors, who wanted only to trade with the Iberians, Carthage had territorial ambitions.

Left: the Moorish court in all its opulence
Right: figures on a Roman tomb, the Alcázar museum

Muslim Spain

For a long time after the Reconquest – really until after the death of Franco – the standard version of Spanish history portrayed the Muslim period as an unwanted occupation by an alien Arabic and North African culture that forcibly imposed its religion and values on an unwilling populace. The reality is far more complex. The successive waves of Muslim 'invaders' were never a homogenous bunch and culturally they merged with the indigenous population while at the same time showing tolerance for other religions. After centuries of co-habitation and social evolution, the last 'Moors' could claim to be ethnically just as Spanish as the crusading unifiers from the north, even if they held to a minority faith. Interestingly, since the restoration of democracy in Spain, many people in Andalucia have converted to Islam, claiming that they are merely returning to the traditions that their ancestors were forced to give up.

These were bound to conflict with the grand designs of Rome. Between 264 and 241 BC, Carthage lost almost all its Iberian colonies, and by the end of the Second Punic War (219–201 BC) its power base on the peninsula had been destroyed completely.

Roman construction in the area demonstrated its dominance and the physical imposition of its centralised rule over the new province. *Hispania Ulterior*, part of which was renamed *Baetica*, corresponded to today's Andalucía. Corduba (Córdoba), its administrative capital, became the peninsula's largest and richest city. Roads and aqueducts were constructed, and new cities, such as Acinipo near Ronda (whose ruins barely hint at its past glory), rose in the province. Málaga's Roman theatre exemplifies the empire's grandeur. Archaeological finds in the Marbella area hint at a Roman presence in the 1st-century BC; Marbella may have been the site of the Silniana settlement. Remnants of a bathhouse that was part of a larger complex can be seen near San Pedro de Alcántara's beach, and ruins of a Roman villa remain at the mouth of the Río Verde.

Famous Andalusian Romans

The emperors Trajan and Hadrian, the philosopher Seneca, writers Lucan and Martial, and Ossius, originator of the Nicene Creed, were among the list of illustrious Andalusian-born Romans. The Hispano-Romans spoke a language and lived by legal codes that formed the basis for those used in Spain today. In Baetica, a productive agricultural region, an indulgent ruling class

enjoyed the high life in towns and on *latifundias* (extensive estates) worked by slaves. It was a pattern that would recur throughout the region's history.

By 400, Christianity was the state religion and the Roman Empire was in decline, bringing fresh invasions from central Europe. Andalucía was occupied by the notorious Vandals; one theory holds that the name 'Andalucía' derives from the Moorish for 'land of the Vandals'. A few years later, the Germanic Visigoths, adherents of the Aryan Christianity of Byzantium, arrived on the peninsula as allies of Rome to drive out the invaders. The Visigoths encountered little opposition when in 468 they claimed Rome's Iberian provinces for themselves. The Visigoths adopted the local form of Latin and much of Roman law, and in 586 they made Catholicism their state religion. Their nobles were in constant dispute over the election of kings – in 297 years of sovereignty on the peninsula, there were 33 monarchs, few of whom died of natural causes. They never really mingled with the majority Hispano-Roman population, who tended to distrust their Germanic overlords. This distance from the natives, together with a propensity for high-level intrigues (from which the Church was not excluded), created the ideal conditions for another invasion, this time by the Muslims of North Africa, in 711.

Muslim Invasion

After an initial force landed at Gibraltar and went on to defeat the Visigoth King Roderick, an army of some 50,000 Muslims arrived. The majority were Berbers from present-day Morocco, but it was the Syrians and Arab leaders who laid the foundations for the administration, language, culture and aristocracy of their newly conquered realm, which they named Al-Andalus. Disaffected Hispano-Romans, as well as Jews, welcomed the Moors, who rapidly took control of the entire peninsula except for a handful of rebellious pockets in northern Spain and the Basque country, where Christian resistance was the greatest.

Meanwhile in Damascus, the ruling Omayyad dynasty was overthrown. Its sole survivor made his way to Al-Andalus, where, in 756, he established himself as Abd al-Rahman I, with Córdoba as his capital. He began building a state in which there was considerable religious tolerance and patronage of learning and culture. In many places the Moors built on what already existed. Málaga's Alcazaba has examples of horseshoe arches – a Visigoth development – supported by Roman columns. Stones from what may have been a Roman temple were used to build the Alcazar of Marbella in the 10th century.

Abd al-Rahman III began his reign with a series of military campaigns against the Christians who were proving to be a nuisance on the northern borders. In 929, now secure in his royal tenure, he declared himself caliph, ushering in the most glorious period of Al-Andalus. In the whole Western world, Córdoba had no equal as a city, in size, splendour, culture and learning.

Left: the cultured Moors loved poetry and music
Right: a Moorish depiction of the biblical fight between David and Goliath

It would be difficult to overestimate the Moors' contribution to Andalusian culture. They introduced everything from Greek philosophy to the Arabic numbers that replaced the clumsy Roman numerals; they invented that quintessential Spanish musical instrument, the guitar; and they gave many words to the language, of which examples such as alcohol, cotton, saffron, algebra, coffee, zenith and zero later passed into English. They also introduced oranges and lemons, sugar cane and apricots, and countless herbs and spices.

Hakam II continued the enlightened and effective rule of his father but, as had been the case with the Romans and Visigoths, the upper classes lost interest in everything but their privilege and pleasure, while the masses became increasingly discontented. During most of the reign of the weak Hisham II, the militarist Almansur was the caliphate's most powerful ruler. He imposed civic discipline, initiated public works and waged successful campaigns against the Christian kingdoms, ransacking Barcelona, León and the pilgrimage city of Santiago de Compostela.

Following the death of Hisham II, the Caliphate sank into disarray. By 1031 it had splintered into 26 small kingdoms called *taifas*. This division between people is still felt in Andalucía today. Seville, the most powerful kingdom, was a stronghold of Andalusies – Muslims of Arab or Spanish descent born in Al-Andalus. Málaga, Marbella, much of the south coast and Antequera were to become part of the kingdom of Granada, a Berber bastion of the Moorish presence in Al-Andalus for another 460 years.

Christians Fight Back

Some *taifas* sought security as vassals of Christian kingdoms. These kingdoms, inspired by an increasing degree of mutual cooperation, an upsurge in religious zeal, and disunity among the Muslims, stepped up the momentum of their 'reconquest' of the peninsula. After Toledo fell to Christians in 1085, Sevilla and other *taifas* summoned the help of the Almoravids. This puritanical north African sect beat back the Christians, and then decided to stay and subjugate Al-Andalus. Their harsh rule soon proved odious to the free-thinking Spanish Moors, and terrifying for Christians and Jews. Some 60 years later the Almohads, a marginally more tolerant sect, ousted their north African rivals. They revived a failing economy, encouraged serious scholarship and constructed fine buildings, of which Seville's Giralda tower is a shining example.

The Christian victory at the battle of Las Navas de Tolosa in 1212 tolled the death knell for the Almohads and signalled the end of Muslim dominance in Al-Andalus as, one after another, their major centres fell to Christian forces. Soon only one kingdom

The Moorish Legacy

Systems of water management still used today, and a variety of crops, fruit and herbs are among the Moors' significant legacies. Fine Moorish architecture is most grandly on show in the magnificent Mezquita of Córdoba and Granada's glorious Alhambra. In the Gothic, baroque and Renaissance buildings that were to come, it is often the addition of delicate *mudéjar* craftsmanship in wood, ceramics or stucco that is the most noteworthy feature. Moorish domestic architecture has persisted over centuries and has in modern times been adapted to meet the needs of today's urban builders: clustered villages with cube houses resemble Berber communities in north Africa; the Roman *atrium* serves as a central patio providing privacy, shade, colour and bubbling water; and, in the narrow streets, the buildings themselves act as sun shades.

remained: Granada, which also encompassed most of the province of Málaga. For nearly 250 years its Nasrid dynasty maintained independent rule by paying tribute to Christian Castile. The Nasrids were responsible for initiating the building of the Alhambra palace which, by 1390, Mohammed V had polished into the architectural marvel we see today.

The rest of Andalucía was parcelled out to Christian knights, some of whom were honoured with titles and very large *latifundia* estates. This echo of the land division of Roman times laid the groundwork for agrarian neglect and social injustice, which persisted through the centuries. Many Muslims sought refuge in Granada. Those who stayed in Christian territory, the Mudejars, worked as artisans, craftsmen and agricultural labourers, but, as with the Jews who served in the professions, it was hard for them to move up the social ladder without incurring the resentment of Christian citizens.

Ferdinand and Isabela

Following their marriage in 1469, Ferdinand of Aragon and Isabela of Castile ruled Christian Spain in partnership. They set out to conquer the country's last Moorish bastion and in 1485 their forces took Marbella; after a long siege, Málaga succumbed two years later; Boabdil, the last Nasrid king, surrendered Granada in 1492 and the Reconquest was complete. The subsequent persecution and banishment of Muslims and Jews, the most accomplished agriculturists and administrators, gravely damaged the region's economy.

It was in 1492 that Cristóbal Colón (Christopher Columbus) sailed from Andalucía and first landed in the Americas, sparking off the Spanish conquest of the New World. Much of the wealth shipped back from America was spent in an explosion of grand building. The cathedrals of Málaga and Granada are some of the great religious buildings of that time.

Above: Sala de Embajadores in the Alhambra, Granada
Right: Queen Isabela of Castile

Andalucía benefited little from Spain's new, powerful status. As poor Andalusians headed for the Americas to seek their fortune, farming estates fell into neglect. Bandits preyed on travellers and the coast was vulnerable to raids by north African pirates. For centuries, neglect, stagnation and poverty were the rule in much of Andalucía. The whole region suffered terribly during the Civil War (1936–9) and in the subsequent 'Years of Hunger'.

The Coast Today

Under Franco, whose dictatorship lasted for 35 years after the civil war, civil liberties were repressed. But the decision to allow US military bases on Spanish soil opened the door for foreign investors and visitors. Torremolinos became a fashionable resort, and Alfonso von Hohenlohe's exclusive Marbella Club catered to the rich and titled. The Costa del Sol was born.

In the 1960s, the first package tourists landed at Málaga airport. Building and catering for foreigners became the area's biggest economic activities, farms were given over to high-rise hotels, and farmers became waiters.

Today the number of expats in the region is well into six figures.

Franco's death in 1975, the accession of King Juan Carlos, the reinstatement of democracy and subsequent entry into the European Community ushered in a new prosperity, as can be seen especially in the new motorways and main roads that have vastly improved communications across the region.

The Costa del Sol, today, however, is having to come to terms with decades of more or less unchecked urban sprawl. In 2006 a massive town planning corruption scandal erupted in Marbella, shocking both the police and central government into belated action.

The 'Cinderella' Resort

Marbella had a rudimentary economy based on smallholdings, fishing and iron mining when, in the early 1950s, the marquis Don Ricardo Soriano opened some chalets and a *venta* in El Fuerte. Wealthy friends and family came to stay, including his nephew, Prince Alfonso von Hohenlohe of Liechtenstein. The prince bought a fig plantation and also a *cortijo* which he transformed and opened as the Marbella Club in 1953. It set the tone for Marbella's development as a somewhat exclusive holiday resort and residential area. Other centres along the Costa del Sol opted to serve the mass market, and are now regretting it.

Above: modern Andalusians

HISTORY HIGHLIGHTS

20,000–1,000BC Prehistoric cave-dwellers populate southeastern Spain; Iberians arrive from north Africa. Mining becomes important in the Bronze Age; the fabulously rich state of Tartessos is founded near Huelva. Phoenician traders introduce the modern concepts of writing and money.

500BC Carthaginians displace the Greeks, and sack Tartessos.

201BC Rome triumphs in Second Punic War and consolidates its sovereignty throughout the Iberian peninsula.

1st century AD The Roman province of Baetica, with Córdoba as its capital, makes munificent contributions to the empire's food supply and wealth.

400 Roman Empire in rapid decline; Germanic tribes invade the peninsula. Vandals reach the south and are chased into north Africa by the Visigoths, Rome's allies.

475 Rome concedes Visigothic rule in its Iberian provinces.

711 The Visigoth King Roderick is defeated by a Muslim force from north Africa led by Tarik.

756 Abd al-Rahman I founds the Omayyad dynasty in Córdoba and becomes the first ruler of the Muslim al-Andalus.

929 Abd al-Rahman III proclaims an independent caliphate; al-Andalus reaching its zenith.

1212 The military defeat at Las Navas de Tolosa is decisive in the decline of Muslim power.

1492 Christian Spain's *annus mirabilis*: Granada, last Muslim kingdom, falls; Columbus reaches America; Jews are banished.

1600 Much of Spain's great wealth is depleted by Carlos V and Felipe II in European territorial struggles and in fighting the Reformation; culturally Spain enters its golden age. Writers Cervantes and Lope de Vega are at the peak of their powers, the Andalusian painters Velázquez and Murillo are making their names; Cano and other architects develop their baroque style.

1700 Spain's last Hapsburg king dies; Europe is plunged into the War of the Spanish Succession, from which the Bourbon Felipe V eventually emerges triumphant. The 18th century is marked by two wars with Britain.

1808–14 During the Spanish War of Independence, Napoleon's armies help themselves to Iberia's art treasures.

1900 Spain has lost all of its colonies. Reform movements in Andalucía are ruthlessly subdued.

1931 After permitting the dictator Primo de Rivera to run the country for seven years, Alfonso XIII flees the country and a republic is declared.

1936 A National Front government fails to stem political chaos. General Franco assumes the leadership of an uprising to which fellow-fascists Hitler and Mussolini lend their support.

1939 The end of a terrible three-year civil war, from which Franco emerges as the country's undisputed ruler.

1953 The US signs a defence pact with Franco; the advent of modern tourism.

1975 King Juan Carlos I begins to shepherd Spain towards democracy and into the European fold.

1982 Socialist Felipe González heads the government.

1991 The maverick independent Jesús Gil sweeps the board in Marbella's mayoral elections, ushering in a new period of regional optimism.

2002 The euro replaces the Spanish peseta as the main unit of currency.

2004 Socialist government returned to power in March.

2006 Property development corruption scandal rocks Marbella council.

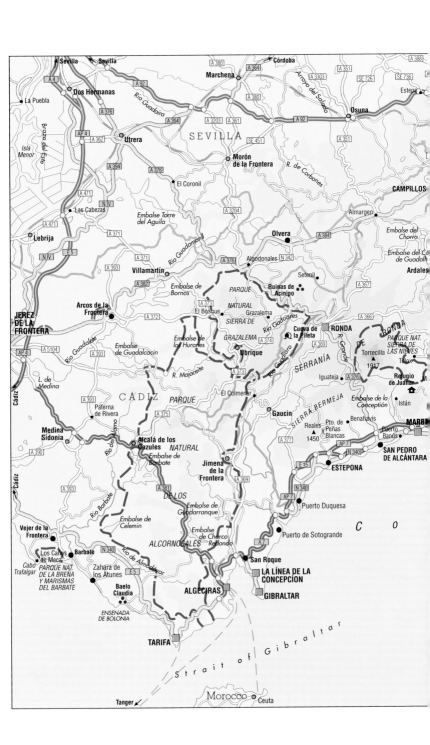

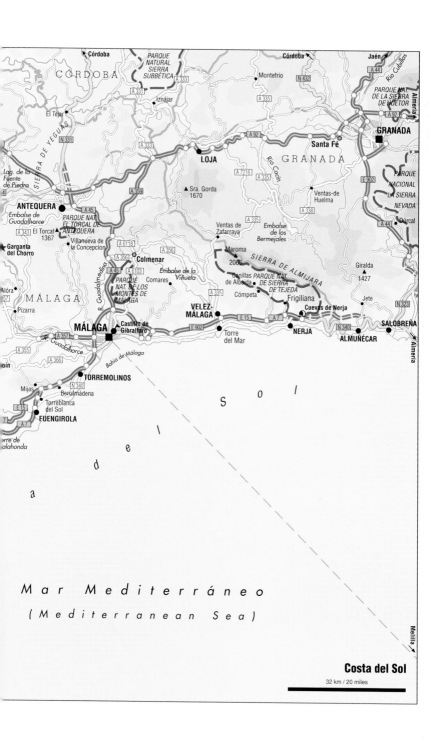

Costa del Sol

32 km / 20 miles

itineraries

Orientation

The Costa del Sol is Spain's most famous strip of coast. For five decades it has managed to accommodate both upmarket and mass-market tourism with flair and ease. Its miles of sandy beaches and sunny climate are the biggest attractions, along with an incredible number of bars, restaurants and nightclubs. For many visitors, the uninhibited holiday atmosphere is all they come for and all they need.

But there is another side to the 'Costa del Sol', a marketing nickname for the the coast of the province of Málaga, part of the autonomous region of Andalucía. This privileged belt of Mediterranean shoreline has an immensely long history and an accumulation of cultural treasures to show for it. Surprisingly, perhaps, when you see the unending estates of villas and apartments, it also has some great, unspoilt countryside to explore.

Finding your Way Around

The premise for this guide is that you will be spending about a week somewhere on the Costa del Sol, and, while you want to spend some or most of your time in the sea or on the sand, you would also like to get out and see other things. The 19 routes described in detail in this book will take you to all the best places within reach of the coast, offering half-day, full-day and overnight trips. Each itinerary (complemented by a practical section at the back of the book) contains suggestions of where to eat and drink and, when appropriate, where to stay.

For simplicity, all the routes depart from Marbella, although the suggested itineraries can easily be adapted to start from wherever you happen to be staying. The first two itineraries revolve around Marbella itself: two easy half days to get you acclimatised. These are followed by a trip into the historic port-city of Málaga, birthplace of Pablo Picasso, and a tour into the hills to see the spectacularly sited town of Ronda. If you don't feel like driving, there is a scenic railway line that reaches Ronda as well. The next few trips take you along the coast and inland but never too far away from the main heartland of the Costa del Sol. The final few routes cover more distance, taking you well away from the tourist resorts into some corners of Andalucía that are well worth the trouble of getting to know.

Left: Nerja, the archetypal Andalusian village
Right: sandy beach near Marbella

1. DISCOVERING MARBELLA *(see map, p24)*

Despite the brash modernity hemming it in on all sides, Marbella has a delightful old town centre of narrow, pedestrianised streets and shady alleyways full of flowers and other colourful details. You can take a leisurely stroll around this route in an hour but you'll probably want to take longer to allow for window shopping and people watching. Add a couple of stops in bars and cafés along the way and you could stretch this walk out to fill a whole morning or afternoon.

Start the walk from Marbella's central spine, Avenida Ramón y Cajal, by walking up the main access-way into the old town, Calle Huerta Chica. Follow this street as it kinks right and becomes pedestrianised in front of Restaurante La Pesquera (part of a chain of seafood restaurants in which you can choose your meal from the fish tank; tel: 952-765-170), into Plaza de la Victoria. Continue in the same direction across the square on Calle de la Estación and you will reach the **Plaza de los Naranjos**,

the centre of the old town and of Marbella itself. This square was laid out in the 16th century in a deliberately regular manner, in contrast to the erratic Moorish streets and alleys around it. It is named after the orange trees planted in the middle of the square (which are joined by some exotic trees and shrubs). On three sides of the square

Above: Plaza de los Naranjos
Left: a relaxing way to travel

are bar and restaurant tables, which are good for a coffee or aperitif at any time of day.

The main building overlooking the square is the **Ayuntamiento** (Town Hall) with the tourist information office occupying one corner of it. Also of note is the **Casa del Corregidor** (Chief Magistrate's House) built in 1552; it has a stone portico in Gothic-*mudéjar* style, an attractive iron balcony and a Renaissance gallery above. The ground floor is occupied by the Restaurante Ciaboga (tel: 952-773-743). The regular shape of the square is broken in the southwest corner by a chapel, the 15th-century **Ermita de Santiago** (labelled Cofradia del S. Cristo del Amor), the first church built in Marbella. Its odd orientation suggests that it was built before the rest of the square was conceived.

Ancient Origins

Leave the Plaza de los Naranjos by the street opposite the Casa del Corregidor, Calle General Chincilla, which brings you quickly to a sloping whitewashed wall. Above this looms Marbella's old Arabic wall, the earliest parts of it dating from the 9th century. Turn right here along Calle Carmen into the square beside Marbella's main church, the **Iglesia de Nuestra Señora de la Encarnación**, which dates from the 17th century. Turn immediately left, following the city wall (the lowest stones here are thought to be of Roman origin) along the dog-legged Calle Trinidad. At the next crossroads turn right down Calle Salinas and first left to visit the **Museo del Grabado Contemporáneo** (Museum of Contemporary Engraving; summer: Tues–Sat 10am–2pm, 7–9pm; winter: 10am–2pm, 5.30–8.30pm). It is housed in a Renaissance building, the Hospital de Bazán, with a handsome gallery on the uppermost floor. The collection inside includes works by Miró and Picasso.

Retrace your steps to the end of Calle Trinidad and carry straight on up Calle Salinas, with the city walls on your left. You emerge briefly on Calle Arte, stepping for a moment outside the old town. In front of you is the start of an elongated triangle of gardens, the Parque Arroyo de la Represa, in which stands the **Museo del Bonsai** (Bonsai Museum; summer: daily 10.30am–1.30pm, 5–8pm; winter: 10.30am–1.30pm, 4–7pm), which is noted especially for its collection of dwarf wild olive trees.

Take the flight of steps to your left, passing a shrine in a rock overhang, and you enter Plaza Castillo. There is only one way out of this – into the adjacent Plaza de Bernabé. Continue straight across this square and descend the broad flight of steps into Calle Carmen (the street which you came along earlier). Turn right up Calle Ortíz de Molinillos, which turns sharp left beneath a statue of the Virgin Mary set into the wall of El Balcón de la

Above: the tiny, 16th-century Capilla de San Juan de Dios

Virgen restaurant (tel: 952-776-092) to become Calle Remedios. This brings you to Plaza Puente de Ronda, the site of one of the city's old gateways.

Turn right up Calle Ancha, which is the main street of the Barrio Alto, a 'new town' laid out in straight lines beyond the city walls after the conquest of Marbella in 1485. There are some handsome houses lining the street. On the way up, on the right, you pass two narrow alleys, which are filled with pots of flowering plants: these are calles Montenebros and Principe. Continue as far as the pretty Plaza del Santo Cristo, named after the church that stands on it and which has a distinctive blue-and-white chequered spire. If you would like an Andalucian finale to your day, you can come back to this square later for the show at Flamenco Ana María (tel: 952-775-646), beside the church.

Double back down Calle Ancha and turn right down Calle Princesa. At the end, turn left down Calle Aduar. This brings you back to the Plaza Puente de Ronda. From here it is a short walk back to the Plaza de los Naranjos, via the alleyway of Pasaje Cruz.

Towards the Sea

Cross the Plaza de los Naranjos and leave it by the street next to the chapel, Pasaje Valdés. Turn right at the bottom and left out of the Plaza Africa on Calle Africa. Here you leave the old town. Ahead of you, across Avenida Ramón y Cajal (the arterial avenue from which you started the walk), is the fountain in the middle of **Paseo de la Alameda**, a park characterised by its attractive, if crumbling, ceramic benches. Carry on straight across it and you will be heading down **Avenida del Mar**, lined with statues cast from moulds made by Salvador Dalí, towards Marbella's seafront. There are plenty of restaurants along here, but you might want to return to the old town for lunch or dinner.

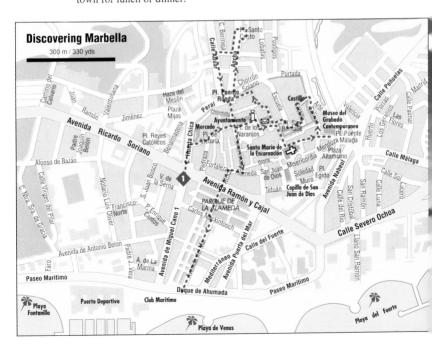

2. A DRIVE AROUND MARBELLA *(see map, p43)*

Fabulous wealth and sometimes questionable taste come together on Marbella's so-called 'Golden Mile', connecting the town centre with the jet-set marina at Puerto Banús. This morning-long route is a look at how the other half lives, finishing with lunch in the more down-to-earth hill village of Benahavís.

Before setting out you might want to reserve at table in one of the restaurants in Benahavís. This is essential at weekends and peak holiday times but mid-week or off-season you can usually find somewhere to eat when you get there. If you get off to a late start you can always go straight to Benahavís for lunch and visit Puerto Banús on the way back.

Leave Marbella on the N340 dual carriageway along the 'Golden Mile'. A short way after the coppery spire that rises from the traffic island in the middle of Plaza Monseñor Rodrigo Bocanegra (a roundabout universally known as El Piruli) you pass the **Marbella Club** on your left and, immediately after it, **Puente Romano**. Although ostensibly hotels that aspire to offer grand luxury, they are more like artificial, self-contained villages dedicated to the pampering of the rich. You're welcome to stop and step into the public areas, have a drink or a meal, or temporarily join a 'beach club', which will entitle you to lounge by the pool and have lunch from a buffet of good things to eat and drink.

The oldest of the two establishments is Marbella Club (www.marbella club.com, tel: 952-822-211), which grew out of the private residence of Prince Alfonso von Hohenlohe. As the number of the prince's guests grew in the

Above: Puerto Banús

1950s, he turned his home into an exclusive club in which luxury was defined, in his words, as 'a blend of privacy and gardens'.

The Puente Romano (www.puenteromano. com, tel: 952-820-900), next door, is built around a small Roman bridge that once stood on the Via Augusta linking Cádiz with Rome.

Diagonally across the road from the Puente Romano is Marbella's mosque, the sparkling white **Mezquita del Rey Abdulaziz** (Sat–Wed 7–9pm).

Just before you get to Puerto Banús, you could turn off into Urbanización Coral Beach to visit one of Marbella's more interesting museums, the **Museo Ralli** (Jun–Sept: Tues– Sat 11.30am–2pm, 6.30– 10pm; Oct– May: 11.30am– 2pm, 5– 8pm), one of four art galleries scattered around the world run by a nonprofitmaking organisation that exists to promote European and Latin American art.

Puerto Banús

When you get to the turn off into **Puerto Banús**, follow the signs under the dual carriageway and straight across the roundabout that is adorned with a sculpture of a green rhinoceros. At the roundabout at the seafront, turn right and park where you can, on or near Avenida Julio Iglesias (named after one of Spain's most internationally famous pop singers) to visit the marina of the wealthy across the road. As well as a place to berth your boat, Puerto Banús is also a shopping centre with a good choice of bars and restaurants. Two popular places for a drink, if you decide to

come back later, are the Sinatra Bar at the far end of the seafront, and Salduba next door.

Resuming your journey, continue parallel to the seafront and turn right at the roundabout with a fountain, and go up the short Bulevar de las Estrellas (Boulevard of the Stars). To get back on to the N340 dual-carriageway going west (towards Estepona and Algeciras) you need to go underneath it and double back at the next roundabout.

Leaving Puerto Banús behind, you quickly come to San Pedro de Alcántara, officially part of Marbella but a mere shadow of the more fashionable parts of the resort. Its main virtue is that its seafront, away to your left, is relatively unbuilt up by the standards of the Costa del Sol.

Benahavís

Continue under the bridge indicating the Marbella boundary, cross the dry Río Guadalmina and take a right turn to Benahavís just before entering Estepona. A little road takes you past the Atalaya Golf and Country Club and under the motorway. For a few minutes you slip into rural Spain and the excesses of the concrete coast feel far away. Suddenly you are in a landscape of fig, carob, pine and evergreen oak trees and you might just see a herd of grazing goats. The road winds into the hills up a short but pleasant canyon, Las Angosturas, that promises even more remoteness from modernity, but it is not long before you reach **Benahavís**, a white village becoming shrouded by apartment blocks. With around 25 restaurants, Benahavís promotes itself as a 'culinary capital' of the Costa del Sol and this is the main reason to come here. You can stroll around and look at the menu boards for an appetising and inexpensive *menú del día* or you can plump for one of the better known but pricier restaurants. Among the latter are the Hotel Amanhavís (Calle del Pilar 3; tel: 952-856-026) and the Gran Hotel Benahavís (tel: 902-504-862), a mini-Andalucian village standing below and apart from the rest of the town.

There is not much else to do in Benahavís except eat and browse in the town's few shops, although there are a couple of art galleries to visit, most notably that of metalworking sculptor David Marshall, which is located in the village-within-a-village that he created, La Aldea.

Further progress into the hinterland is checked by the unpassable bulk of the Sierra Bermeja, which rises to over 1,400m (4,500ft) behind the town, and the only thing to do after lunch is retrace yours steps down the canyon, under the motorway and back on the N340 along the coast to Marbella. You can always make a stopover at Puerto Banús if you missed it earlier or if you fancy a drink and a stroll as the sun goes down.

Above Left: traditional boat, Puerto Banús. **Left:** catching up on the news
Right: simple tomato salad

3. MALAGA *(see map below)*

Sightseeing and shopping in the provincial capital, taking in the splendid cathedral. Visit the Museo Picasso, walk to the house where the artist was born, then tour the Moorish Alcazaba. Have lunch in Málaga or in the Parador overlooking the city, then explore the exotic botanical garden of La Concepción.

You can drive from Marbella to Málaga in an hour, or less if you take the A7 toll motorway.

Approaching the city outskirts along the N340, follow signs to Málaga-Centro Ciudad, which will lead you into Avenida Andalucía. When you see a line of modern commercial buildings, look for the large **El Corte Inglés** department store ahead on the left. Bear right, around the traffic island to pass in front of the building and take the first right to its underground car park.

Walk back to Avenida Andalucía and turn left along it to cross the bridge over the Río Guadalmedina to Alameda Principal. If you are interested in modern Spanish art, you may like to visit the new **Centro de Arte Contemporáneo** (Tues–Sun 10am–8pm), which is reached by turning right along Calle Comandante Benitez on the far side of the bridge. Calle Alemania, where the museum is located, is just off Comandante Benitez . The museum's late opening hours mean you could pay it a visit at the end of your day.

Back on Alameda Principal, keep left and then turn left into Calle Torregorda. Ahead you will see the **Puerta de Atarazanas**, an 11th-century Moorish entrance to what is now Málaga's food market. Walk through to the other end and go straight ahead until you reach the river. On your right, in Paseo de Santa Isabel, is the **Museo de Artes y Tradiciones Populares** (Mon–Fri 10am–1.30pm, 4–7pm, Sat 10am–1.30pm). The delightful building, dating from 1632, used to be an inn run by Franciscan monks. It is now

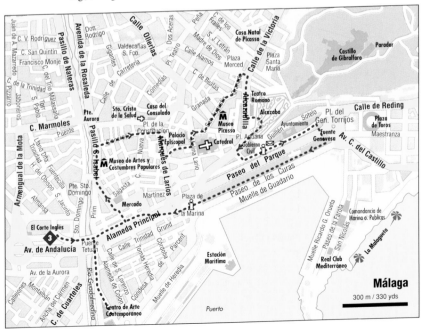

a museum of arts and popular traditions, occupying three floors around a central patio.

Turn right when leaving, take the first right into Calle Cisneros and continue into Plaza de la Constitución, site of a stamp and coin market on Sunday. Notable on the north side is the **Casa del Consulado**. To the left, the **Iglesia del Santo Cristo de la Salud**, inaugurated in 1630, features typical Spanish Mannerist elements. Leave the plaza on the right and head into Calle Marqués de Larios, the city's main shopping street since 1886. Its construction was financed largely by the Larios family, which made its fortune from gin.

A Crippled Cathedral

Take a left turn into calles Strachan and Salinas and you will find yourself in front of the **Catedral** (Mon–Fri 10am–6.45pm, Sat 10am–5.45pm; entrance at the side), with the elaborate façade of the **Palacio Episcopal** on your left. Work on the cathedral was begun, in Gothic style, in 1528, on the site of a former mosque. Several style changes followed and in 1782 the building evolved into what you see today. The cathedral is popularly known as *La Manquita* (The Cripple) because its second tower was never completed. The story goes that funds needed for it were diverted to support the American War of Independence. Inside, the most exceptional feature is the *coro* (choir), completed in 1662 by Pedro de Mena. The 40 tableaux in mahogany, cedar and red ebony are marvellously detailed. Other highlights include the Gothic Chapel of St Barbara, to the right of the central chapel of the apse. Adjoining the cathedral is the **Museo Catredralicio**, featuring religious art.

Walk along the left side of the cathedral, noting the elaborate carving on the portal and, on your left, that of the **Iglesia del Sagrario**, the surviving section of a Gothic church built in 1488. Turn left into Calle San Agustín. Midway along the cobbled street you will see the palace of the Condes de Buenavista, built in 1530–40. The austere exterior and watchtower give the building an unusual martial appearance. Inside, it is graced by a beautiful patio. The building once housed a museum of fine art, which closed to make way for a museum devoted to Málaga's most famous son, Pablo Picasso. The **Museo Picasso** (Tues–Thur and Sun 10am–8pm, Fri–Sat 10am–9pm) displays 155 of the artist's works donated by his daughter-in-law and grandson. In the basement of the building are ruins of Phoenecian Málaga.

Above: *La Manquita*
Right: modern art in Málaga

At the end of Calle San Agustín, turn right into pedestrianised Calle Granada, which takes you to the Plaza de la Merced. On the far corner of the square is the restored **Casa Natal de Picasso** (Mon–Sat 10am–8pm, Sun 10am–2pm; tel: 952-060-215), where Picasso was born in 1881. It now houses the Picasso Foundation, containing a reference library and rooms for temporary exhibitions. It is well worth seeing but don't confuse it with the Picasso Museum.

Cross the square again, past the Astoria cinema, and turn right into the pedestrianised Calle Alcazabilla. Cross over for a look at the restored **Teatro Romano** (Wed–Sat 10am–2.30pm, 4–7pm, Sun 10am–2.30pm), built during the reign of Augustus and discovered by chance in the 1950s. Then go into the **Alcazaba** (summer: Tues–Sun 9.30am–8pm; winter: 8.30am–7pm). In the 8th century the Moors began building a fortress on the remains of a fort left by the Romans. It is connected by a rampart to the Castillo de Gibralfaro *(see below)*, a Moorish construction on Phoenician foundations, at the top of the hill. What you see of the Alcazaba today is for the most part a construction ordered by a king of the *taifa* of Granada in 1057, which was renovated in 1933. This is an introduction to typical features of Moorish architecture: double walls with defensive towers surround gardens, patios and palaces.

Go left when leaving the Alcazaba. The solid square building on your right is the old **Aduana** (customs), constructed for the port authorities in 1829 but which now houses the central government's delegation in Málaga province. When you reach the tree-lined Paseo del Parque, continue left past the neo-baroque **Ayuntamiento** (Town Hall), completed in 1919. The building's decorative features allude to the city's economic activities at the time. Tourism did not feature then and does not much now. You come to Plaza del General Torrijos and the **Fuente Genovesa**, a Renaissance fountain. One block east of the plaza is Málaga's **Plaza de Toros**, built in 1874. The area between the bullring and the seafront, called **La Malagueta**, has many good eating places and bars. Try one of the seafood houses in the area and possibly order *fritura malagueña*, a mixed fish fry that is a local speciality. Alternatively, the **Café de Paris** (Calle Velez Málaga, 8; tel: 952-225-043), not far from the lighthouse, is one of the city's best restaurants.

Elegant Gardens

Return to the city centre along the **Paseo del Parque**, elegant gardens with 2,000 species of flowers and trees, many identified with ceramic plaques. You could lunch at one of the restaurants off Calle Marqués de Larios, such as the **Restaurante Chinitas** (Calle Moreno Monroy 4; tel: 952-210-972) or try a selection

Left: taking a stroll in Málaga

of *tapas* from the 75-plus choice at **Bar Logueno** across the road at Calle Marín García.

Excursion to Gibralfaro

Before leaving the city, you might like to make a short excursion by car up to the **Castillo de Gibralfaro**. You can get there on foot from the Alcazaba, but it is more comfortable to drive. (There is also a bus, No. 35, from the city centre, but it is infrequent.) The route is rather devious but it is signposted. When you have collected your car, find your way down the broad avenue you have just walked along, the Paseo del Parque and from the roundabout of Plaza del General Torrijos take Paseo del Reding, signposted for Almeria and Gibralfaro. This is the old main road along the coast east of Málaga and it follows the base of the mount on which the castle stands. Look out for the signs left for Gibralfaro, which take you winding through housing estates to the top of the hill. Just before you reach the castle itself you'll see a turning left to the **Parador** (tel: 952-221-902), a hotel with an incomparable setting, looking down over the bullring and harbour, making it a great place for lunch. The views are even better from the walls of the castle itself (daily 9am–8pm, till 6pm in winter), taking in the whole of the city centre. As a bonus, the grounds of the castle have been turned into a botanical garden: most of the species of plants you see were grown by the Arabs.

A Pretty Marina

Málaga likes to say that it is a city of botanical gardens, and it has some grounds for this claim. A guided visit to **La Concepción Botanical Garden** (Tues–Sun 10am–dusk), on the northern outskirts of Málaga, is a pleasant way to spend the afternoon. At one time the private garden of a wealthy family, it has a large collection of exotic plants and palm trees. To get there, follow signs to Antequera until you reach the turn-off signposted to the Jardín Histórico Botánico La Concepción.

Above: the Gibralfaro

4. RONDA *(see maps, pp33 & 43)*

A scenic drive inland to Ronda, one of Spain's most spectacularly sited
towns. If you want to stay the night and go horse riding in the hills the
following morning (details from Ronda's tourist office), or head on to
Tarifa *(see Itinerary 15, page 56)*, Ronda has lots of hotels, including
the luxurious Parador perched above the Tajo (Gorge).

*Allowing for a few stops to enjoy the views and take photographs, you can
comfortably drive to Ronda from Marbella in 1½ hours.*

It's a good idea to arrive by 10.30am – the light is better for photography
on the outward journey, before the heat haze sets in. At the eastern end of
San Pedro de Alcántara, turn off the N340 onto the A376, signposted to
Ronda. About 8km (5 miles) from the turn-off, a valley on the left is now **Los
Arqueros Golf Course**, designed by Seve Ballesteros. Clinging to a hillside on the right are the pretty pastel-coloured buildings of La Heredia, a
modern *pueblo*-style residential complex. After that comes the luxury residential area of **El Madroñal** and **El Coto** (tel: 952-786-688; www.buenas-
mesas.com), a hunting lodge-style restaurant specialising in meat and game.

The wide road is in good condition, but its twists and turns reduce the
recommended speed limit to about 50kph (30mph). Smashed crash barriers
testify to the fate of drivers who have exceeded it. In early summer, vivid
yellow gorse covers the lower slopes. On the left are grand views across
the valley of the Río Guadalmina and undulating hills towards the coast
and Gibraltar and, perhaps, Africa. You might spot eagles and vultures soaring
above the region, where the mountainside is at its starkest in the Serranía
de Ronda, part of the **Parque Natural Sierra de las Nieves**. After about
35km (22 miles) you are on the high plateau of the Serranía, the road is less
twisting, and your average speed can
rise to 80kph (50mph). Isolated ham-
lets lie in the basins of the Genal and
Guadiaro rivers on the left. Shortly
afterwards Ronda looms into view.

The town sits atop a rocky outcrop
in a basin surrounded by the mountains
of the Serranía de Ronda. It is 740m
(2,428ft) above sea level, the highest
of the mountains reaching almost
2,000m (6,562ft).

Bandit Country

Banditry was common here. The Serranía's nooks and crannies provided
perfect hiding places for outlaws, who
would come down from the hills to
hold up a stagecoach or kidnap the son
of a wealthy landowner. *Bandoleros*
and tobacco smugglers were active in
the area right up to the 1950s, and to-

Left: the Tajo and Puente Nuevo

day their dubious story is told in Ronda's **Museo del Bandolero** (Calle Armiñan 65; daily 10.30am–7.30pm).

Stop before entering the town to look at the two gateways in the town's remaining walls. **Puerta de Almocabar**, on the right, was built in the 13th century and gave access to the Moors' *alcazaba* and town; **Puerta de Carlos V** is a typical Renaissance gateway. The wall's remnants run round to the right. Drive into the town and through the old part, to which you will return on foot. Cross the Puente Nuevo into the newer part of town and try to find parking. The best bet is to go through the **Plaza de España** into Calle Virgen de la Paz and take the first left to a public car park. If it's full, continue along Calle Virgen de la Paz to find a space in Plaza de la Merced. Walk back to Plaza de España and pop into the tourist office for relevant information.

Across the Gorge

Ahead is the **Puente Nuevo** (New Bridge) spanning the **Tajo** (Gorge) across the Río Guadalevín and overlooked by a parador occupying the site of the old Town Hall. The bridge, built in 1751–93, reaches 98m (320ft). The architect of what has become the town's symbol is said to have died for his hat. As he was being lowered in a basket to inspect his creation, the wind caught his hat. He reached out for it and fell into the gorge. The Tajo is an impressive sight that seems to hold a compelling fascination for people intent on suicide. Picadors' horses that were gored and killed by bulls used to be pushed into the gorge here. There is now a visitors' centre built into the bridge (Mon–Fri 10am–6pm, Sat 10am–1.45pm, 3–5.30pm, Sun 9am–2.30pm).

Across the bridge, you are again in the old part of town, La Ciudad. Turn left into Calle Santo Domingo. On the left, **La Casa del Rey Moro** was not the house of a Moorish king, as the name suggests, but was built in the

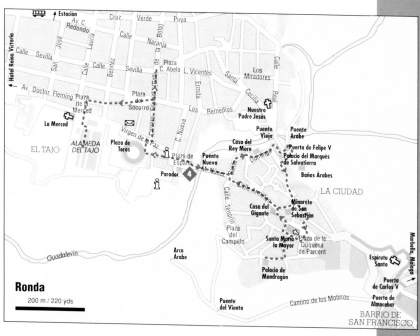

18th century as the town house of a wealthy family. Its attractive gardens are open to the public (daily 10am–7pm). A secret tunnel with a long, winding stairway, the Mina de Ronda, leads down to the bottom of the gorge. When under siege, the Moors used Christian slaves to carry buckets of water up these stairs. Also noteworthy are the elaborate façade, sculptured balcony and wrought-ironwork of the privately owned **Palacio del Marqués de Salvatierra**, which dates from the 18th century. The wrought iron here is typical of the work of Ronda's renowned forges: you will see much more of it around town in *rejas* (window-bar grilles) of doorways and on balconies.

Moorish Baths and Palaces

Continue left through the **Puerta de Felipe V**, a small triumphal arch built in 1742 commemorating Spain's first Bourbon king. Down the slope is the **Puente Viejo** (Old Bridge), built in 1616. From here you have an impressive upward view of the Tajo on the left. To the right is the **Puente Arabe**, definitely Moorish but perhaps originally Roman. Further right, the **Baños Arabes** (Mon–Fri 10am–6pm, Sat 10am–1.45pm, 3–5.30pm, Sun 9am–2.30pm) have the typical roof shape of Arab baths. Built in the 13th century, the baths are in a fairly good state of preservation, but conservation work continues sporadically, so they are sometimes closed. Go back up to the Puerta de Felipe V and bear left up Calle Marqués de Salvatierra.

As you turn right into Calle Armiñán, the main street, you will see on the left the 14th-century **Minarete de San Sebastián**, which shares the Nazrid architectural style of the magnificent Alhambra palace in Granada. Next along, off to the left and up José María Holdago, is the **Casa del Gigante** (Giant's House), a Moorish palace of the same period but much changed over the centuries. Turn left here to head down the alleys to the 13th-century **Santa María la Mayor** church, which is a converted mosque. A stone's throw southwest is the **Palacio de Mondragón** (Mon–Fri 10am–6pm, Sat 10am–1.45pm, 3–5.30pm, Sun 9am–2.30pm), built in 1314 by the Muslim king of Ronda. Little remains of the original save the underground passages connecting with the *Alcázar* ruins.

Bullfighting Legends

Wander back to and across the Puente Nuevo towards the **Plaza de Toros** (daily 10am–6pm). This bullring, dating from 1785, is one of Spain's oldest. Some 200 years ago, Pedro Romero killed 6,000 bulls here. Below part

Above: Baños Árabes
Right: the Plaza de Toros

itineraries

of the covered terraces is a bullfighting museum. Ernest Hemingway and Orson Welles, both friends of the acclaimed Ronda matador Antonio Ordoñez, were ringside regulars. (Welles' ashes were scattered on the Ordoñez estate.) For more bullfighting memorabilia – including the edible kind, in the form of *rabo de toro* (ox tail) – go to Restaurante Pedro Romero (tel: 952-871-110) opposite the Plaza de Toros. Other lunch options are **El Tragabuches** (Calle José Aparicio 1; tel: 952-190-291), one of Andalucía's finest restaurants; the **Don Miguel** (Calle Villanueva; tel: 952-877-722), which has good views of the Puente Nuevo; and the **Parador** restaurant (tel: 952-877-500) on the Plaza de España.

The Craft Tradition

After lunch, head up La Bola, as the pedestrianised Carrera Espinel is known. Here you will find plenty of shops, including tourist tat. Craft specialities – ironwork and saddlery – tend to be too bulky to carry, but this is a great place to buy leather shoes and boots. Make your way back to **Plaza del Socorro** and turn left to the Plaza de la Merced and into the **Alameda del Tajo**. This park promenade was completed in 1806 with money raised from fines for indecent behaviour and blasphemy. During the civil war Republicans are said to have thrown 512 alleged Nationalist sympathisers from its balcony, though some claim they were hurled into the gorge.

Heading up from the park, you will soon arrive at the **Reina Victoria**. This historic hotel was built by the British in 1906 and has seen better times, but it remains the perfect spot at which to stop for refreshments on the terrace. Take a leisurely stroll through the gardens for dramatic views over the cliff. Back in your car, return across the Puente Nuevo, through La Ciudad and take a right turn as soon as you exit from the town.

If you happen to miss this small road, stop to ask someone for the **Camino de los Molinos**. The road twists and turns through a series of olive groves and finally leads to the spot which is known to have the most impressive, most photographed views of the Tajo and Puente Nuevo. When you've finished clicking your camera, return to the coast the way you came.

5. RONDA BY RAIL *(see maps, pp33 & 43)*

Rail is not the quickest or most direct way to get to Ronda from the Costa del Sol, but the scenic line up that crawls through the hills from Algeciras is a great way to approach the town if you are travelling by public transport or just feel like leaving your car behind. The main towns on the line are also covered in Itineraries 11 and 16.

There are four trains a day in each direction, the first one leaving Algeciras at around 7am, and perhaps the most convenient leaving at 12.10pm (although before you set off you should check the current timetable with the rail company, RENFE, tel: 902-240-202; www.renfe.es).

Algeciras offers the best connections for public transport, but the first part of the line is not attractive and if you have a car it is better to park it at San Roque station or, better, drive a little further to Jimena de la Frontera. To get to either station from Marbella, take the motorway towards Algeciras and turn off at Exit 115 onto the A369 (after the town of San Roque itself) for Jimena de la Frontera. San Roque station is a few kilometres from this turn off, and Jimena station is 33km (20 miles). Wherever you catch the train, take a seat on the right on the way up for the best views.

The Algeciras to Bobadilla railway was driven through the uplands of Cádiz and Málaga in 1892 by a British consortium. Although it was intended to be a main line from central Spain to the coast, it has never been more than a glorious branch-line folly of rail engineering, a slow journey through enchanting scenery, stopping at quaint village stations. As well as serving tourists on the way to Ronda and local people hopping between the villages en route, the train is also used by hikers, who find it a quick and convenient way to get into some great countryside.

Leaving the sprawling industrial conurbation of **Algeciras** and **San Roque**, the lower part of the line crosses flat and gently undulating land, mainly used for cattle. The grazing steers are often accompanied by snow-white egrets stand-

Above: matador statue in Ronda

itineraries

ing motionless on their backs or on the ground at their feet. Leaving San Roque station you may well see an even more conspicuous bird, as there are a number of storks' nests on the electricity pylons. For a long while the railway follows the perimeter of the **Parque Natural de los Alcornocales**, a reserve named after the cork-oak trees that predominate in its scattered woodlands – trees stripped of their bark to shoulder height, leaving the dark sienna heart wood exposed, are a common sight. There is a yard full of neatly stacked cork bark next to the neglected **La Almoraima** station.

Jimena de la Frontera is the first of a series of pretty stations painted white and enlivened with splashes of colour and with orange trees and pot plants on their platforms. Most of these stations are several kilometres from the towns and villages that they nominally serve.

After the tiny request stop of **San Pablo de Buceite** the line follows the valley of the Río Guadiaro all the way to Ronda, crossing imperceptibly from the province of Cádiz into the province of Málaga. Between **Gaucín** and **Cortes de la Frontera** the line passes through a series of 10 tunnels, which come one after the other in quick succession. In between them are glimpses of the pretty river valley that the line follows, and one of the tunnels has a series of arched openings in the middle. If you are vigilant, away to the right you will see the two ends of the **Garganta de las Buitreras**, a deep gorge in the landscape, popular with outdoor adventure enthusiasts. As its names indicates, it is home to a colony of vultures. The train creeps slowly along this stretch of line for good reason. In October 2006 part of a goods train tumbled into the river bed – mercifully without anyone being injured. It was probably derailed by a landslide that had cracked a rail. Cortes de la Frontera itself is perched high on the slopes above the station with peaks reaching almost 1,400 m (4,500 ft) behind it. The next stop is **Jimera de Libar**, which has a restaurant – **Quercus** (tel: 952-180-041), serving Mediterranean food – in the rail shed next to it.

Towards Ronda

After **Benaojoán** the landscape opens up, and the train picks up speed. There is a glimpse of Ronda at one point but otherwise you won't see it until you get there. Rather than heading straight for its destination, the line turns away from it and describes an exaggerated loop to the north to pick up height before turning south for a final climb to the station. Arriving at Ronda, the train has climbed from sea level to 723m (2,370ft) in just over 100km (60 miles).

Ronda station is about 10 minutes' walk from the city centre. The traffic signs tell you to turn right outside the station along Avenida de Andalucía and then left at the end of Calle San José, which will bring you to the bullring, Puente Nuevo and the tourist office; however, you could hack into Route 4 *(see page 32)* directly by going down Calle Doctor Carrillo Guerrero across the road from the station, turning right at Plaza del Ahorro down Calle Setenil and continuing as best you can in this direction across Plaza de los Descalzos to find the Puente Arabe.

If you have time to potter on Andalucía's railways, the line continues from Ronda all the way to Granada. At Bobadilla, half-way and in the middle of nowhere, it connects with the Seville–Málaga line. From here there are also services north to Córdoba and Madrid.

6. ANTEQUERA *(see maps below and p50)*

See the historic architecture in the town and villages of Antequera and visit its small gem of a museum. Enter the lunar landscape of El Torcal before driving through the verdant terrain of the Montes de Málaga.

You can drive to Antequera in about 1½ hours. Take the A7 motorway towards Málaga, then the A45. Some 40km (25 miles) from Málaga, after passing through a number of tunnels, the road reaches the 780-m (2,560-ft) point of Puerto de las Pedrizas and branches off to Antequera (signposted to Seville and Córdoba), then descends, offering views of the agricultural plain.

Cave Tombs

Before entering the town, look out on the right for a sign pointing to the **Conjunto Dolmenico** (Tues–Sat 9am–6pm, Sun 9.30am–2.30pm). There is a car park outside the fenced-off area. Of the two dolmens here, **Cueva de Menga** is more impressive than **Cueva de Viera**. These burial chambers date from around 2500BC and little is known about the people who built them, how they managed to haul the stones, quarried in the mountains, to the site or how they raised them into position. The total weight of the 31 stones is around 1,600 tons; some of the slabs weigh 180 tons. These large cave tombs, which are 25m (82ft) deep and 3.5m (12ft) high, were then sealed and covered with earth. It is assumed they were the burial places of local leaders and their possessions, but looting over the centuries has left no evidence of either. A third dolmen, Cueva del Romera, is 2km (1 mile) away.

A Centre of Humanism

Back in your car, drive into town and follow the signs to the Castillo or Alcazaba. Park near the tourist office and walk up the hill, through the **Arco**

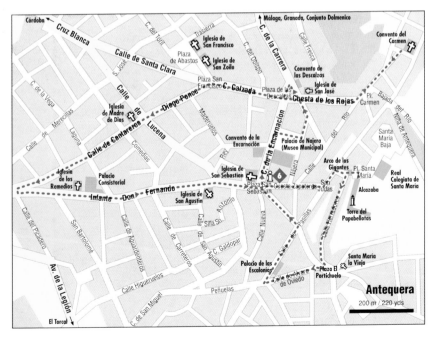

de los Gigantes, a Mannerist building from 1585. Looking back, it gives a picture-frame view of the town and its towers. Ahead is the façade of the **Real Colegiata de Santa María**, a huge church built in 1514–50, where, according to the plaque on its wall, a group of leading Spanish humanists taught, in defiance of theological opposition that argued that the humanistic emphasis on reason, knowledge and the centrality of man in the scheme of things was incompatible with Christian dogma. The recently restored church is now a national monument. From the side of the arch, steps lead up into what remains of the **Alcazaba**, which the Moors built in the 14th century on the remains of a Roman fortress. Now it is mostly a garden overlooked by the belltower of **Torre del Papabellotas** (Father Acorns Tower), built in 1582 with funds from the sale of a cork-oak plot. It was not long after taking the town from the Moors in 1410 that the Christians embarked on a building spree of churches and monasteries.

Look eastward and you see **La Peña de los Enamorados** (Lovers' Peak), which resembles a reclining figure. The peak is associated with a sad love story. Tazgona, daughter of a wealthy Moor from Archidona, was the secret lover of a Christian from Granada, but neither family would permit their marriage. Pursued by her father's men, they climbed the peak and jumped into the abyss to their deaths.

From the Giants' Arch, take a left down Calle Herradores to the mid-18th-century **Plaza El Portichuelo**, which is an ornate baroque affair. The street chapel of Santa María la Vieja, one of numerous churches repaired after the ravages of Napoleon's army, is like many seen in Mexico. In the niche of the high altar, the image of the **Virgen de Socorro** is especially revered by the townsfolk. Along Cuesto Alvaro de Oviedo and right into Pastillas, you will see on the right the **Palacio del Marqués de las Escalonias**, a Mannerist-style palace from the late-16th century that exemplifies the type of town house in whichlocal artistocrats lived. It's worth making an effort to see its Arab-style gardens, which are overlooked by three-floored galleries.

Turn left into Cuesta del Viento, descend a flight of steps, and you pass the

Above: Santa María la Vieja
Right: Arco de los Gigantes

17th-century **Iglesia de Santo Domingo**. Dominating the plaza of the same name is the **Iglesia de San Sebastián**, a 16th-century Renaissance church with a striking baroque-*mudéjar* tower and an interior filled with paintings and sculpture. The plaza's fountain dates from about the same time.

Down to the right of the church, and adjoining it, you will find the 16th-century Carmelite **Convento de la Encarnación**, with notable *mudéjar* work inside. Opposite the convent is the **Palacio de Nájera**, built in the early 18th century for another rich family. Inside is an attractive patio and the **Museo Municipal** (Tues–Fri 10am–1.30pm, Sat 10am–1.30pm, Sun 11am–1.30pm). This small, carefully tended museum has a singular prize: the *Efebo*, a life-size bronze figure of a garlanded boy, which was ploughed up in a field in the 1950s. Dating from the 1st-century AD and probably a copy of a Greek work, it is among the finest Roman statues found in Iberia.

Pagan Mythology

Go left down Calle Nájera, bearing left to the small, pretty Plaza de las Descalzas (Square of the Barefooted), behind which is the **Convento de las Descalzas** of the closed order of Carmelites. The convent's façade, a good example of the particular baroque style found in Antequera, somewhat ironically includes references to pagan mythology in its decoration. Turn up Cuesta de los Rojas, alongside the convent, then head left past the gateway of Postigo de la Estrella to the National Monument of **Convento del Carmen**. This forms the remains of a 1633 Carmelite convent. The rich interior is dominated by three big reredos.

Return to Plaza de las Descalzas, through Calle Calzada, then right, past the market at Plaza San Francisco to the 1515 late-Gothic monument of **Iglesia de San Zoilo**. If you can, go inside to see *mudéjar* plasterwork and the dome. Take Calle Diego Ponce past the 18th-century **Iglesia de la Madre de Dios**, a good example of Andalusian rococo. When you reach the Alameda de Andalucía, turn left into Calle Infante Don Fernando. On the left is a tourist office (usually open during office hours) and the 17th-century **Iglesia de los Remedios**, dedicated to Antequera's patron saint, Nuestra Señora de los Remedios. The church's convent houses the **Palacio Consistorial** (Town Hall) with a 1950s neo-baroque façade and late 17th-century colonnaded cloister.

Turn towards the city centre along the town's principal shopping street, noting the belfry of Iglesia de San Agustín. Cross Plaza San Sebastián into

Above: Iglesia de San Sebastián. **Top Right:** local speciality
Right: Parque Natural El Torcal

itineraries

Cuesta Zapateros and Cuesta San Judas, and up a hill past whitewashed houses to return to your car. For lunch you can sample fine regional dishes at **El Angelote** (tel: 952-703-465) on Plaza Coso Viejo, near the museum. Or head back to your car and follow signs to the **Parador**, whose restaurant (tel: 952-840-261) is also a good option. You could stop first for *tapas* at La Espuela, a bar under the grandstand in Antequera's bullring.

Salt Lake and Highlands

Before returning to the coast from Antequera, you may feel like making a detour north on the motorway towards Seville to see the **Laguna de la Fuente de Piedra**, technically the largest salt lake in Spain, but it doesn't always seem like it, as the quantity of water depends on the season and the weather. The real reason to come is to see the flocks of greater flamingoes that nest here. You should see them at any time beween December and August, but February to June are the best months. There is a visitor reception centre and observation platform just outside the town of Fuente de Piedra.

When you've finished seeing Antequera (and Fuente de Piedra), take the scenic 16-km (10-mile) drive from the city to **El Torcal de Antequera**. In these 1,200ha (2,965 acres) of protected highland you can wander among weird and wonderful limestone formations carved by the elements. There are marked paths, and you are well advised to stick to them – it's easy to get lost in this maze. Ivy, wild irises, phlomis, labiates, herbs and holm oaks are among the varied vegetation. At the end of the road from El Torcal, turn right to **Villanueva de la Concepción**, a sleepy village, and head east to **Casabermeja**, where you can pick up the motorway south to Málaga.

If time allows, you may want to follow signs to the Jardín Histórico Botánico and roam the dense gardens of **La Concepción** *(see page 31)*.

7. A Half-day in Istan *(see map, p43)*

A leisurely morning or afternoon drive to the mountain village of Istán constitutes the perfect introduction to the lovely countryside that lies in surprisingly close proximity to the developed coastal strip.

Turn off the N340 at km177, just west of Puente Romano and the mosque. The 16-km (10-mile) long road (C427) is narrow but should present no problem to cautious drivers. After about 2km (1¼ miles), past the Club Sierra housing estate and the last signs of urbanisation, you begin to get

the impression that you are in the countryside. Big, established villas – good buys when land here was very cheap – are scattered on your left. With the Sierra Blanca rising steeply on the right, the road twists through small folding hills. Avocado and citrus trees make the valley below lush.

Soon the impressive bridge spanning the valley that carries the *autopista* toll road appears, and a bit further beyond that, the wall of the **Embalse de la Concepción**, the dam that supplies water to the coastal communities. Scrubland – some of it terraced – is dotted with juniper, gorse and wild herbs, with pockets of cork-oak and olives. Soon you are in the municipal area of **Istán**. Pine, fig, citrus and carob make an appearance, and in spring, a profusion of wild flowers. The mountain rises on the right, *cortijos* (farm estates) dot the view to the left. Just below Istán, you pass the Ermita de San Miguel in the rockface, to which the villagers make a *romería* (pilgrimage) at the end of September. Don't be put off by the messy buildings on the approach to Istán. You should find parking spaces as you enter the village.

A 9th-century Village

There is not much of note to see in Istán (population 1,300), but a stroll along the narrow, crooked streets gives the impression that this ancient village has changed little in domestic building style and street layout since the 9th century, when it was founded by the Moors. You can hear the burbling sound of running water everywhere. The village still has a functioning system of irrigation channels, which was laid out by the Moors. It's no wonder that the Moors liked the place so much. The village's sole 'monument' is the Torre de Escalante, at the highest point of the village.

Many local people now work on the coast, and fewer till the small plots, tend the valley's citrus trees or herd the sheep and goats that sustained the village until recently. Some run bars whose weekday regulars are retired men, with day-trippers at weekends. Have a drink and absorb some local life before returning to the Marbella road.

Above: the ancient village of Istán

8. LUNCH AT THE REFUGIO DE JUANAR *(see map below)*

A morning drive to the village of Ojén for lunch at a former hunting lodge standing in a beauty spot in the foothills of the Serranía de Ronda.

Turn off the N340 onto the A355 on the eastern edge of Marbella. It's 19km (12 miles) to the Refugio de Juanar. After you've negotiated the outskirts of Marbella, the road twists up between fir and eucalyptus trees. Terraces of citrus trees are stepped down to a *barranco* (ravine) on the right. There's a fine view of the village of **Ojén** as you pass it.

After the village the road twists up to the 580-m (1,900-ft) high Puerto de Ojén pass. Take a turn-off to the left (signposted to Juanar), and the road travels 5.5km (3¼ miles) into the nature reserve's stark landscape. It eventually reaches an oasis of trees surrounding the **Refugio de Juanar** (tel: 95-288-1000). The Refugio was built by the state-run Parador organisation on the foundations of a Larios family *(see Itinerary 3, page 29)* hunting lodge. The staff formed a management cooperative and, with the help of the provincial authorities, they have made it a very comfortable and friendly hostelry, with an attractive pool and terraces. Game is a speciality of the kitchen, and a log fire blazes in the bar in winter (some of the bedrooms also have fireplaces). The menu of the day is excellent value at around €25, and the portions could feed a giant. Alternatively, bar snacks are available.

You can walk off the effects of lunch along the 2.5-km (1½-mile) road to the **mirador**. From here, more than 1,000m (3,281ft) above sea level, there is a fine view over green valleys and hills to Marbella and, sometimes, across to Africa. If you're here at dusk, you might catch a glimpse of the wild ibex that live among the rocky crags and that often descend to drink water. Back at the *refugio*, if you're feeling energetic and have good walking shoes, you could follow part of the forested trails into the Sierra Blanca, to Istán or Ojén.

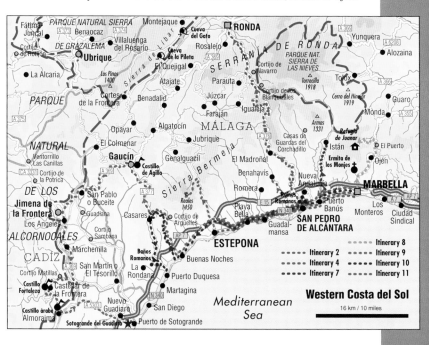

9. A MORNING IN ESTEPONA *(see map, p43)*

A morning trip to Estepona; a drive into the wooded Sierra Bermeja; a visit to Puerto de Estepona; lunch in the country or at the quayside.

It is a quick 25-km (15½-mile) journey west to the town of Estepona from Marbella. Take the coastal N340, not the toll highway. Before you reach the town you will see indications that this is becoming the next trendy area of the Costa del Sol, with fashionable new beachside property developments, golf courses and luxury hotels such as the Las Dunas and the Kempinski.

One attraction that might tempt you to make a detour, especially if you have children with you, is the **Selwo Aventura Wildlife Park** (tel: 902-190-482, www.selwwo.es), a 100-ha (250-acre) reserve, in which 2,000 animals, including lions, tigers, elephants, rhinoceros and other exotic species roam in semi-liberty. Visitors view the resident wildlife from special buses, but to tour the park in full takes the better part of a day, so you might want to save that for a separate outing.

For now, press on into **Estepona**, and park along the Avenida de España, which runs alongside the beach. The tourist office is at the eastern end of the adjoining Paseo Marítimo, if you need any information. Cross over into Calle Santa Ana and wander at will around the old town.

An Immaculate Old Town

There is nothing of particular note in this quarter, but it is pretty and immaculately maintained – whitewashed buildings beneath tiled roofs have flower-filled balconies and solid *rejas* (grilles) across their windows. Street names are painted on ceramic tiles. In the summer cafés put out tables in the attractive **Plaza de las Flores**, once a venue for bullfights. In the Casa de Cultura at its eastern end there may be an exhibition of interest. In Calle Castillo are remnants of the walls of a castle first built by Moors and rebuilt after the Christians took the town in 1456. Behind the ruins is the bustling weekday food market. The town's clock tower symbol, **Torre del Reloj**, remains from a 15th-century church. The nearby replacement parish church of Los Remedios was built in the 18th century. Wander through the back streets, keeping an eye out for art and craft shops.

itineraries

There has been a great deal of residential development in Estepona in recent years. What distinguishes the municipality from others along the coast is the ongoing role of agriculture in the lives of many of its 43,000 residents. Here the development and diversification of agriculture are actively supported by the local authorities. You can see evidence of this on your drive into the Sierra Bermeja. In place of the traditional lemon-growing, more profitable tropical fruits are harvested. A monument on the Paseo Marítimo honours the honest toil of Estepona's farmers and fishermen – the town still has a big fishing fleet.

Back in your car take Calle La Terraza, which dissects the old town and is signposted 'Jubrique'. The road is in a good state of repair and rises through agricultural land to the starker slopes of the Sierra Bermeja and Peñas Blancas pass. About 15km (9 miles) from the town, turn off to **Los Reales** to enter a wooded area where streams burble and roe deer, genets and foxes hide out. Marked paths lead deeper into the woods to pinsapo firs – the classical model of a Christmas tree – that are indigenous to the area and grow only at heights of more than 1,000m (3,280ft). The high point, **Alto Los Reales** (1,450m/ 4,757ft), looks out over the coast 8km (5 miles) away, to Gibraltar and Africa.

Return the same way. About 2km (1¼ miles) before Estepona is the **Venta Los Reales** (tel: 952-802-646), where you can stop for a hearty lunch of unfussy country dishes. Rabbit, cooked in various ways, is a local speciality. Travel through the town and west to **Puerto de Estepona** where the fishing fleet is anchored next to small pleasure craft and ocean-going vessels. The port does not have the glamour of Puerto Banús but is no less attractive for that. On Sunday morning it is the scene of one of the Costa del Sol's liveliest *mercadillos,* with stalls selling arts and crafts, secondhand bric-à-brac, clothes and houseware. If you did not have lunch at Los Reales, you can choose from one of the many restaurants that line the quays. Then it's back to Marbella, unless you decide to combine this trip with Itinerary 6 to Antequera *(see page 38).*

10. A HALF-DAY IN CASARES *(see map, p43)*

A morning or afternoon drive to Casares, one of the country's most-photographed *pueblos*; a dip into the sulphurous waters where Julius Caesar is said to have bathed; lunch or dinner at a laid-back oasis among the vineyards; and, lastly, a look at the *pueblo* port of Puerto Duquesa.

Drive west along the N340 beyond Estepona, past Costa Natura (tel: 952-808-065, www.costanatura.com), Spain's first residential complex for nudists, and, just after the km147 mark, turn right to Casares. The narrow, 14-km (9-mile) road is in fair condition. You are soon transported into a scene that contrasts markedly with the coast's concrete ribbon. Eucalyptus trees line both

Left: Puerto de Estepona
Above: pretty old town

sides of the road before the Sierra Bermeja's heights come into view, their rolling hills scattered with *cortijos* (farm estates).

After 8km (5 miles), the road narrows and rises among cork-oaks. On a bend is the rustic Venta Victoria (tel: 952-894-199). A little further on are good views across to the coast and, after 3km (1¼ miles), around a bend, you will find the town of **Casares**, a confection of white cubes on a mountain spur topped by the brown outline of an *alcazar*. Several roadside restaurant bars, all with pleasant terraces, overlook the town. Further on, turn left and do the locals a big favour by parking at the entrance to their *pueblo*. In Plaza de España, a typical Spanish square, is a statue of Blas Infante. Born in Casares in 1885, Infante led the Andalusian Nationalist movement, for which he was murdered by Franco's supporters. Climb the narrow, uphill roads to see what remains of the **Moorish castle**, or rather, as the ruins don't really amount to much, to check out an excellent vantage point. This is the site from which hundreds of *moriscos* (descendants of the Moors), who revolted against their Christian rulers in the early 16th century, were hurled to their deaths.

Back on the road that skirts the town, follow signposts to Manilva and you start to appreciate a different view of Casares. Soon you see the vineyards of Manilva, which is known for both the quality of its grapes and its lively *vino de terreno*. Near a quarry on the town's edge, take a track on the left (signposted **Baños Romanos**) to the river and travel for about 1.5km (1 mile) to reach the Roman Baths. From the outside, the baths don't look much, but inside there are graceful Roman arches, and the water is invitingly clear. Julius Caesar visited these baths and local people like to believe that its waters' healing powers were responsible for curing his skin problem.

Nearby, the British-run Roman **Oasis** (tel: 952-892-380) is a restaurant (Jun–Sept: evenings, and lunch on Sun). **Manilva** is an unremarkable place, but you may want to visit a backstreet *bodega* (wine cellar) to sample a glass of the local *vino*. Afterwards, continue to the N340, turn right and you will reach the turn-off for **Puerto Duquesa**, another of the Costa del Sol's *pueblo* ports with the usual boutique-style shops, bars and restaurants, and an array of luxury yachts and cruisers.

11. GAUCIN, CASTELLAR AND SOTOGRANDE
(see map, p43)

Lunch in Gaucín at an old *fonda* (inn); drive into Cádiz province; visit the hideaway of Castellar de la Frontera and Sotogrande's marina.

Follow Itinerary 9 *(see page 44)* to Casares. From the road that skirts the village, turn right on the A377, signposted Gaucín. Be sure to drive carefully along the narrow 16-km (10-mile) road, which, although easily navi-

Above: even locals stop to admire the views
Right: Gaucín village and castle

gable, can be treacherous. Falcons fly above the hushed and starkly beautiful land as the road meanders down to the Río Genal and then up the other side to **Gaucín**, which sits high above the valley.

Park whererever you can find a space in the village. One of the main sights is the 13th-century Moorish **Castillo de Aguila** (daily 10.30am–1.30pm, 6–8pm; winter: 4–6pm). In 1848 the powder magazine blew up and destroyed much of the place. Gúzman el Bueno, defender of Tarifa, died here fighting the Moors in 1309. The church features a much-revered image of the Child Jesus.

Although it has only 2,000 inhabitants, Gaucín has over 10 hotels and pensiones, and around 20 restaurants. One of the more interesting places to stay or eat is the Hotel Fructuosa (Calle Convento 67, tel: 952-151-072, www.lafructuosa.com), a house in the middle of the village. It has a perfectly preserved wine press on the ground floor and a restaurant terrace with great views.

Bull Country

Leave Gaucín on the A369 signposted Algeciras and 2km (1¼ miles) and look back to catch a wonderful view of the village. The road drops through gorse and grass-covered hills past picturesque *cortijos* (farm estates), near which horses and cattle shelter. After 13km (8 miles) the road enters Cádiz province and crosses the Río Guadiaro. This is bull-raising country: about 3km (1¼ miles) after the hamlet of San Pablo you see a bull ranch on the left. The white profile of **Jimena de la Frontera** is outlined against a hill topped by a ruined castle. Quite a few foreigners in search of the real Spain have settled around the village, in the process affecting the 'authenticity' of what they sought.

Continue south on the A369 past meadows where cattle graze and through avenues of eucalyptus trees, until, 14km (8¾ miles) from Jimena, there's a tiny road to the right leading to **Castellar de la Frontera**. The villagers abandoned this isolated place when Nuevo Castellar was built on the main road. The remains of a frontier castle that once proved to be pivotal in the struggle between Christians and Arabs broods over the newcomers' hideaway and the waters of the Embalse de Guadarranque reservoir. A narrow but very scenic road weaves southward to the A369.

Turn left and head into Nuevo Castellar, from where you can pick up a back road to Sotogrande. At the N340 coastal highway, go left (east) and then right at the sign to **Puerto de Sotogrande**. The marina's 'modern Mediterranean' style is quite different from the other *puertos* (ports) on the Costa. Here you may want to have a drink and watch the sun go down over Gibraltar. It's an easy run of 50km (31 miles) back to Marbella.

12. ARDALES, LAKES AND EL CHORRO *(see map, p50)*

This itinerary, taking in Carratraca's spa, lunch in the lake district, and a visit to the spectacular El Chorro gorge, includes particularly fine scenery.

Follow Itinerary 8 *(see page 43)* to Ojén. Between Ojén and Monda the road passes through a stark landscape and a small gorge. Some 19km (11¾ miles) from Marbella is the sleepy village of **Monda**, where elderly locals watch life pass by from the Bar Central. The village is overlooked by a castle-like structure on a hill; this luxury hotel, the 23-room **Castillo de Monda** (tel: 952-457-142, www.castillodemonda.es), was created by two Englishmen, and the St George Cross occasionally flies over the ramparts. The building incorporates the remains of the original Moorish fortress, including an 8th-century tower.

Coín (pop: 18,000), described by one Moorish writer as 'a beautiful place with lots of springs, trees and fruit', is 10km (6¼ miles) on. The terracing and irrigation of the fertile surrounding area are legacies of the Moors. The local people socialise on the tree-lined *rambla* (avenue). Park nearby if you want a to wander around for a while. The maze of narrow streets follows the old Moorish layout; new and old buildings are juxtaposed; the churches Santa María (once a mosque) and San Juan Bautista are of *mudéjar*-Renaissance style.

Above: the remains of a frontier castle dominate Castellar de la Frontera

itineraries

Museum in a Farmhouse

Leave Coín on the A355 to Cártama (take the Málaga road), passing through varied countryside. Across the Río Guadalhorce, turn left on the MA402 and head up the fertile valley where citrus and avocados grow. Near workaday Pizarra, in a converted farmhouse adjacent to an excellent restaurant, is the **Museo de Pizarra** (Mon–Fri 10am–2pm, 4–8pm; tel: 952-483-237), formerly known as the **Museo Hollander**, which has archaeological remains, Spanish antiques and various curiosities accumulated by the American painter Gino Hollander, who lived in these parts some years ago.

As you leave Pizarra, the outline of **Alora**'s castle appears above the white houses that drip down the hill on either side. Phoenicians, Romans, Vandals, Moors and Christians all played a role in the castle's history. Although Alora's many new buildings are evidence of its increased, agriculture-based prosperity, it retains much of its character. It took the entire 17th century to finish the construction of its enormous church, the second-largest in Málaga province.

From Alora head west towards Ardales, taking a scenic drive through the rugged Sierra de Alcaparain and Sierra de Aguas. Turn right for **Carratraca**, which was developed in the 19th century on the site of the *'cortijo* of foul smelling waters' to become a spa for the rich and famous. Some 600 litres (132 gallons) per minute of sulphurous waters, recommended to ease respiratory and skin complaints, gush from the ground at around 16°C (61°F). Byron and Alexandre Dumas, who made the arduous journey over the mountains to take the cures, stayed at the **Hotel El Príncipe** (tel: 952-458-071), built on the orders of Spain's King Fernando VII in the 19th century. After a period in the doldrums, the hotel has now been restored.

Continue through a landscape of almond and olive trees and soon **Ardales** presents a striking aspect against hills on the left. Above the white houses the ochre outlines of its castle and the *mudéjar* tower of its church stand proud. Though the Romans built the first bridge across the river below, Ardales's roots go back much further – prehistoric paintings were discovered in local caves in 1821. To protect the cave's fragile environment, visits are limited. Call the Ardales museum (tel: 952-458-046, www.cuevadeardales. com) for information.

Bear right at the junction after the town and soon you are in Málaga's lake district. Three reservoirs fed by the Guadalhorce and other rivers supply much of the province's water. Continue through pine trees into the **Parque de Ardales**, a recreation park. **Restaurante El Mirador**, (tel: 952-458-203) above a small tunnel, is an

Right: the striking aspect of Ardales

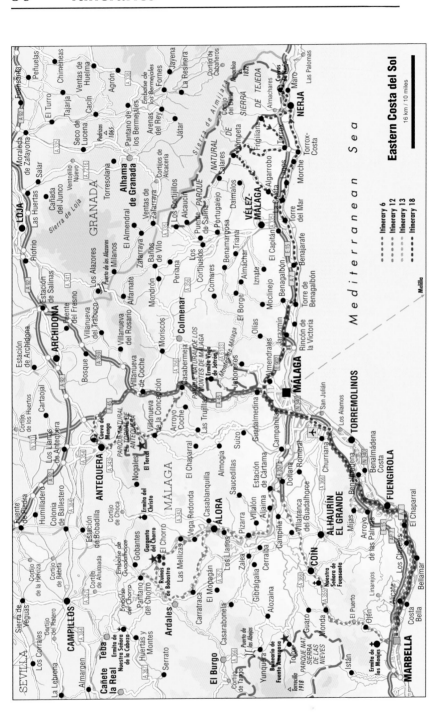

Eastern Costa del Sol

16 km / 10 miles

········· Itinerary 6
━ ━ ━ Itinerary 12
·········· Itinerary 13
▪▪▪▪▪ Itinerary 18

unpretentious place for lunch and has a good view of the reservoir. Further on, across a dam wall, is the smarter and pricier **Mesón el Oasis** (tel: 952-112-400), adjoined by the small, comfortable La Posada del Conde hotel. Note the stone seat from which Alfonso XIII opened the Guadalhorce dam scheme in 1921.

A Church Shaped from Rock

Back at the T-junction go left and a few kilometres on turn right for a 6-km (3¾-mile) drive up to the 600-m (1,968-ft) high **Ruinas de Bobastro**. In the 9th century this was Omar Al-Hafsun's fortress when he rebelled against Córdoba. A special feature is the *mozarabe* church shaped from the rock.

Drive downhill to **El Chorro**; on the left a wooden catwalk hangs from the cliffside. Stop when you see the entrance to the deep cleft of **La Garganta** (The Throat), which is popular with rock climbers. The **Camino del Rey** (King's Pathway) catwalk was built for Alfonso XIII when he opened the dam, but it is now closed for safety reasons. Continue towards Alora. On the way back to Marbella via Estación de Cártama, either go via Coín or turn left to Churriana and the N 340. You could link up with Itinerary 13 *(see below)*, and take in Torremolinos.

13. MIJAS, BENALMADENA AND TORREMOLINOS *(see map, p50)*

Heading from Marbella towards Málaga takes you through a string of resorts that may lack the glamour you leave behind but which have several points of interest, particularly if you have children. This short route links up the best of them. It starts with the hillside village of Mijas, includes a stop for spiritual succour, and ends with the nightlife of Torremolinos, the epitome of mass tourism.

Take the N340 dual carriageway from Marbella to Fuengirola. After passing the lighthouse on the Punta de Calaburra you arrive at Fuengirola, the road curving around the fortress of **Castillo Sohail**, a relatively recent construction. A fort was built on this site by the Moors in the 10th century but was destroyed by Christians, when they took the town in 1485. The castle you see today was built in 1730 to help control illicit trade with Gibraltar.

Fuengirola itself is of little interest although it holds two good open-air markets on Tuesday (the *mercadillo*) and Saturday morning (the coast's biggest fleamarket). You might also want to go into Fuengirola to take the kids to the **zoo** (Avenida Camilo José Cela; open from 10am daily).

Otherwise, ignore the turnings into town and take the one marked 'Mijas Pueblo', which feeds you on to an 8-km (5-mile) road that climbs steeply up the hillside to a roundabout outside the village. Turn left here to visit old Mijas (as opposed to 'Mijas Costa' on the coast below), a curious blend of authentic *malagueño* village and international community – foreign

Above: a farmer poses in front of his olive trees

residents here now outnumber locals. Park where you can, although tour coaches may dictate the space available. If you don't feel like walking, you can always take one of the village's *burro* (donkey) taxis.

Walk through the attractive Plaza de la Constitución and past the small **Plaza de Toros** to the parish church, which has some *mudéjar* features. From the gardens beyond, you can look over the Campo de Mijas, crowded with villa complexes and golf courses, to see Fuengirola and the coast. Back near the car park is an odd museum, the **Museo Carromato de Max** (daily 10am–10pm, winter: till 7pm), with a collection of the tiniest things imaginable, such as *The Last Supper* painted on a grain of rice.

Back in your car, return to the roundabout at the entrance to Mijas and carry straight on over it for Benalmádena, on a road that stays fairly level, high above the sea, through an area of villas and abandoned terraces. Eventually the road drops down and passes under the motorway. Turn left at the roundabout, still following the signs to Benalmádena. Round a corner you see the golden spire of the **Estupa de la Iluminación** (Enlightenement Stupa), Europe's largest stupa (sacred Buddhist monument), which has a soothing silhouette among the ever-expanding housing estates of the coast. The spire rises to 33m (108ft) and is filled with sacred objects, which are intended to remain sealed inside forever. There's a car park next to the stupa, and, even if you aren't interested in religious buildings, it is worth stopping to admire the panoramic view over the coast from the balcony here. Inside the stupa is a light and airy prayer hall overlooked by a serene statue of the Buddha. Around the walls are paintings by a Nepalese artists depicting the life story of the Buddha Sakyamuni.

Benalmádena

Resume the road you were on and carry on for **Benalmádena**. When the road forks among the shops of Benalmádena's old town, take the high road and remain on it when the road forks again next to a filling station. Go straight over the next two roundabouts and this will bring you into Arroyo de la Miel (a subdivision of Benalmádena) and a roundabout next to which stands **Tivoli World** amusement park (opening times vary throughout the year, so check before visiting; open weekends and holidays only between May and mid-Sept; tel 952-577-016).

Next door to Tivoli World is the base station of the **Teleférico** (cable car; operates 10am–6pm, later in spring and summer; closed mid-Jan–mid-Feb) which will whisk you up to the summit of Monte Calamorro at 800m (2,625ft) above sea level, where there is a cafeteria from which a series of rambling paths begin, and offer walkers views over a long stretch of coast. Also on the top of the mountain is the **Jardín de las Aguilas**, a wildlife centre that breeds and displays birds of prey.

You can end the route here by going back on the same road until you pick up the blue motorway signs for Algeciras, and return to Marbella that way. But you may as well finish the day with a night out. Follow the signs from the roundabout outside Tivoli towards Torremolinos. These will lead you down to the seafront of Arroyo de la Miel. Next to the marina is another attraction for children, **Sea Life Aquarium** (daily from 10am). Not

Right: central Torremolinos

itineraries

far away, on Parque de la Paloma, is the dolphinarium, **Selwo Marina** (daily 10am–6pm, later in summer; closed Nov–Feb).

Torremolinos

A dual carriageway leads you into the adjoining, long-established resort of **Torremolinos**, which is cheaper and less pretentious than Marbella. You could follow the signs leading right off the road as you enter, to **Playa de Carihuela**, to stroll along a promenade lined with fish restaurants. The town centre is a little way from here, and it's best to get back in your car afterwards and park somewhere on or near Avenida Palma de Mallorca or, better, Calle Casablanca.

Crossing Casablanca is the pedestrianised **Calle San Miguel**, which, like its surrounding streets and arcades, is packed with shops, cafés and restaurants. At the seaward end of San Miguel is a 14th-century Moorish *torre* (tower). Winding steeply down from the tower, the **Cuesta del Tajo** passes through what remains of the original fishing village. On the way is the 16th-century **Molino de Rosario**, one survivor of numerous flour mills that were fed by a stream, since diverted. It is from the *torre* and the *molinos* that the town got its name. At the end of the walkway is Playa Bajondillo.

There is plenty to distract you for the evening on this stretch of the Costa del Sol, whether you are with children or not. Among the options are Torremolinos' **Magic Palace** (Calle Cuba 3, tel: 952-058-852), which, as the name suggests, is a magic show; or try a flamenco performance in **Pepe López** (Plaza Gamba Alegre, tel: 952-381-284). Alternatively, backtrack to Belamádena, where you can enjoy the multiple delights of **Torrequemada Casino** (Avenida del Sol, tel 952-446-000) instead.

Wherever you end up spending the evening, when you have had enough, all you have to do is look out for and follow the motorway signs in the direction of Algeciras to get back to Marbella.

14. A DAY IN GIBRALTAR *(see map below)*

Experience Gibraltar's unique mix of British and Mediterranean culture – drink draught beer at an English pub along Main Street; take a cable-car ride to see the apes, St Michael's Cave and the top of the Rock.

Drive west along the N340 and soon you will see the unmistakable profile of the British colony of Gibraltar – a 5 x 1-km (3 x ½-mile) lump of limestone attached to the southern tip of the Iberian peninsula. Once you have passed Sotogrande, look for the turn-off to La Línea – Spain's border with the Rock. Leave your car in the guarded car park – there is little point in taking it into Gibraltar's narrow streets – and cross the border on foot. Don't forget to bring your passport with you.

Once there, you can take an Official Rock Tour, either by minibus or by taxi. The 1½-hour itinerary covers all the main sights. Alternatively, take one of the waiting buses or taxis to Market Place, where you will see the **Casemates Gate** – part of the huge fortifications complex that has protected the colony through the many sieges in its history.

Moorish Namesake

Gibraltar (population: 28,750) takes its name from Jebel Tarik (Tarik's Mountain), after the Moorish chieftain whose arrival in 711 sparked the Muslim conquest of Spain. The Moors ruled the town until 1462, when it was captured by the Castilians. The Rock was taken by the British

Above: the Rock in profile

in 1704 in the Spanish War of Succession, and it became a British colony under the Treaty of Utrecht in 1713.

Cross Casemates Square to the foot of Main Street, the principal artery of Gibraltar town. On this pedestrian, shop-lined street you'll be able to appreciate Gibraltar's curious mixture of Mediterranean and British cultures. The locals slip seamlessly between English and Spanish, and taverns selling Spanish-style *tapas* stand shoulder-to-shoulder with pubs whose barmaids pull pints of English draught beer. Walk up Main Street until you reach the Anglican Cathedral, and bear right down Bomb House Lane to the **Gibraltar Museum** (Mon–Fri 10am–6pm, Sat 10am–2pm) whose exhibits relate to the history of the colony. As is the case everywhere in Gibraltar, military history predominates, but part of the building is given over to the restored 14th-century Moorish baths. Among the items on display are a copy of the first evidence of Neanderthal man ever discovered – the skull of a woman, which was found in Gibraltar in 1848.

Make your way back towards Main Street and continue south, through the Southport Gates. On the right is the small, shaded **Trafalgar Cemetery**, where British casualties of the 1805 naval Battle of Trafalgar are buried. But the remains of Admiral Nelson, who died of wounds in the battle, were preserved in a barrel of brandy and shipped back to England.

Apes' Den

Heading along Red Sands Road you come to the cable-car terminal. The cable car (daily 9.30am–5.45pm) takes you to the **Upper Rock Nature Reserve**, with a stop at **Apes' Den** halfway up. This is the place to see the renowned Gibraltar apes, the only wild monkeys in Europe. According to tradition, Britain will lose Gibraltar only when the apes leave. No less a figure than Winston Churchill ordered their preservation during World War II.

A short walk from here is **St Michael's Cave**, the largest of the Rock's many caves. North of Apes' Den, along Queen's Road, you come to the Upper Galleries, or **Great Siege Tunnel**. The galleries were hacked out of the rock to enable Gibraltar's defenders to mount their cannons there during the siege – the fourteenth endured by the Rock – by French and Spanish troops in 1779–83. Return to Apes' Den and take the cable car up to the summit of the Rock for an unbeatable view, with the mountains of North Africa looming across the Strait of Gibraltar. The vista shows you why Gibraltar has played such an important strategic role: here Africa meets Europe, and the Mediterranean meets the Atlantic.

The cable car takes you back to Gibraltar town. Stop at one of the Main Street bars for a pint and some typical pub grub before returning to La Línea and your car. You can link up with Itinerary 17 (*see page 62*) to explore the Cádiz coast beyond the Strait of Gibraltar.

Above: the views from Gibraltar are great, if the Barbary apes let you see them

15. TARIFA, WINDSURFING CAPITAL *(see map, p58)*

Head for the southernmost tip of the Iberian peninsula and enjoy the wide, sandy beaches of the country's windsurfing capital of Tarifa before seeing the Roman ruins of Baelo Claudia on Cádiz's Costa de la Luz.

Take the N340 or the toll motorway west from Marbella, bypassing Estepona and Sotogrande. The unmistakable profile of the Rock of Gibraltar *(see Itinerary 14, page 54)* rises ahead as the road nears Algeciras. You will want to get through the industrial mess around Algeciras, and indeed the town itself, as fast as possible. Once past Algeciras the road starts to round the Strait of Gibraltar– the southernmost tip of Spain – through forests of cork-oaks, with the mountains of north Africa visible across the water. Each autumn hundreds of thousands of birds, including a multitude of vultures and eagles, congregate here as they prepare to make the crossing over the Strait to their wintering grounds in Africa. As you drive along, enormous wind-driven turbines indicate that you are approaching the wind capital of Spain.

Sacrifice of a Son

Winter winds from the southwest or northeast can reach up to 120kph (75mph). Even the average wind speed in the village of **Tarifa**, the continent's windiest spot, reaches a brisk 32kph (20mph). Incessant wind is supposed to affect

Above: kite-surfing
Left: Guzmán el Bueno would not surrender

a person's mental balance and one wonders how the locals hang on to their sanity. Or do they?

Perhaps it was a particularly windy day in 1294 when Guzmán el Bueno (The Good) demonstrated his determination to hold on to the town: he offered to sacrifice his son to the Moors rather than surrender. A Christian traitor had taken Guzmán's eldest son hostage on behalf of the Moors, who offered to hand him back if the town capitulated. Ensconced in his castle, Guzmán threw down his own dagger saying, 'Let my son be killed with an honourable weapon'. The son was indeed killed, the town relieved by Christian reinforcements, and Guzmán was rewarded with large tracts of land and honours that included the founding of the aristocratic Medina Sidonia line. The current holder of the title is a left-wing duchess.

The fortifications and the solid 10th-century **Castillo de Guzmán** castle (currently closed for restoration) illustrate the strategic importance that the town enjoyed in former times. A world apart from the resorts east of Algeciras, Tarifa is a characterful and attractive town. A boon in water sports, especially windsurfing, has helped enliven the narrow streets, which now feature any number of interesting shops, bars, restaurants and tanned, athletic young people. Its port is also a base for scuba-diving activities and dolphin-spotting excursions in summer.

Windsurfer Hangouts

If you want to absorb Tarifa's pleasant ambience at greater leisure, you could stay at one of the town's small inns. For a more upscale choice of accommodation, there are plenty of alternatives further along the coast. These include popular windsurfer hangouts such as the aptly named Hurricane Hotel (tel: 956-684-919, www.hotelhurricane.com). At the long and lovely **Los Lances** beach – behind which are flourishing pine woods – there are hotels, campsites, bars, eateries and, for enthusiasts who throng to the most highly rated and challenging place for the sport in Europe, windsurfing schools and specialist shops.

Take the main road (N340) from Tarifa. After 15km (10 miles) turn off left towards Bolonia and the Roman ruins of **Baelo Claudia** (Jun–Sept: Tues–Sat 10am–8pm; Oct, Mar–May: 10am–7pm; Nov–Feb: till 6pm, Sun 10am–2pm all year) on the left. In the heyday of the Roman empire, Baelo Claudia was a prosperous town devoted to salt-

Right: pretty Tarifa backstreet

ing fish and making *garum*, a sharp sauce from fermented fish that was all the rage in ancient Rome.

Return to the N340 and continue north through farmland dotted with wind turbines; at the next major crossroads go left to Zahara de los Atunes, which is largely dependent on the big bluefin tuna that are netted as they make the annual migration from the Atlantic into the Strait of Gibraltar. A magnificent sandy beach stretches south beyond the luxury Atlanterra development, which is particularly popular with German tourists.

From Zahara, the road hugs the coast to Barbate. Negotiate your way through the town to the modern fishing port where a road, still following the coast, climbs through thick pinewoods, then descends to **Los Caños de Meca**. Nudists in particular enjoy the lovely pine-backed beaches here. From Los Caños you could make a detour to the **Cabo de Trafalgar** (Cape of Trafalgar), off which Britain's AdmiralNelson defeated the Franco-Spanish fleet in 1805 in the battle in which he was mortally wounded.

A Franciscan Monastery

From here, take the scenic road inland to reach the high-perched white town of **Vejer de la Frontera**. Although the modern world has not been allowed to make any significant inroads, the Franciscan monastery has been converted into a small hotel with a restaurant that serves tasty local dishes (**Hotel Convento de San Francisco**, tel: 956-451-001, www.tugasa.com).

From Vejer return to the main N340. Either turn left, to drive on to Cádiz and link up with Itinerary 17 *(see page 62)*, or head back towards the Costa del Sol. If you haven't eaten, you could dine in style at the elegant restaurant at the **Montenmedio Country Club** (tel: 956-451-216) just beyond Vejer. Alternatively, the café at the club's riding centre serves more modest fare. Either way, sign up for a horse-drawn-carriage tour of the country club's estate.

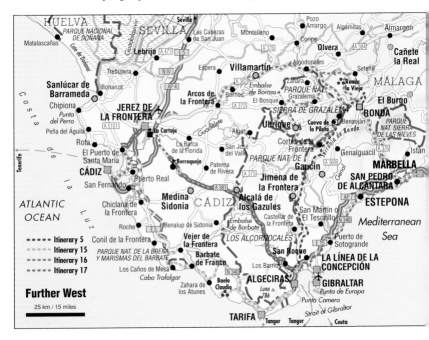

itineraries

16. MOUNTAIN VILLAGES *(see map, p58)*

See Roman ruins, beautiful mountain scenery and prehistoric cave paintings, and shop for crafts. Stay overnight in Grazalema, a base for hiking in the Sierra de Grazalema, at either the Villa Turistica, a luxurious hotel on the outskirts of the village, or at the excellent, inexpensive Casa de las Piedras.

Follow Itinerary 4 *(see page 32)* to **Ronda**. After admiring the town and having lunch, take the A376 road signposted to Seville. After just a few kilometres, turn right at the sign for **Ronda la Vieja**. Following a scenic drive, look out for signs to the Roman settlement of Acinipo and its reconstructed theatre. About 8km (5 miles) on is the unusual sight of a town squeezed into a cleft. Many of **Setenil**'s houses have roofs formed by the overhanging rock, which also provides shade for the streets. One can only hope that the rock remains firmly in place. Backtrack a little way and take the road to El Gastor through some peaceful countryside. Turn left (heading in the direction of Ronda) when you reach the A376 and after 3km (1¾ miles) turn right onto a minor road that leads to **Grazalema**.

This is one of Spain's prettiest mountain villages, and its wettest. Rain-filled clouds, borne on Atlantic winds, billow up against El Torrejón and other peaks as they release their load. In some years the rainfall exceeds 3,000mm (120in). Grazalema is also a popular base for hikers. You can get information about walks in the area from the tourist office in the centre of the village.

The Villa Turistica (tel: 956-132-136, www.tugasa.com), one of the suggested overnight stops, has great views, a swimming pool and offers self-catering accommodation. Alternatively try the comfortable Casa de las Piedras (tel: 956-132-014, www.casadelaspiedras.net) in the centre of the village – both have good restaurants. Other places to eat include El Tajo (tel: 956-132-186), next to the municipal pool, which has wonderful views; and the more simple Zulema bar (Calle Agua 44, tel: 956-132-402).

Blankets and Goat's Cheese

Wool weaving was once an important local industry – Grazalema was known for the high quality of its cloth and *mantas* (blankets) – and in the past decade various initiatives have tried to revive this skill. You can find out more at the **Artesanía Textil de Grazalema** (Mon–Thur 8am–2pm, 3–6.30pm;

Right: a view from Grazalema

tel: 956-132-008), a museum-factory to the right as you enter the village. Opposite the camping site on the road to El Bosque you will find a factory that manufactures a product that has made the village famous far beyond the surrounding *sierras* (mountain ranges). Grazalema's *queso de cabra* is a hard, goat's-milk cheese – a small, round, yellow cheese – and makes a tasty gift.

Along the 18km (11¼ miles) to **El Bosque** the road passes through a stunningly beautiful mountain landscape. Above 1,000m (3,280ft) are pinsapo firs that occur naturally nowhere else in Europe. In other parts are pines, cork-oaks, almonds, olives, carobs, poplars and eucalyptus. Past the hamlet of Benamahoma the road descends more steeply to reach a junction at which you turn right towards El Bosque. Look out for the Los Nogales

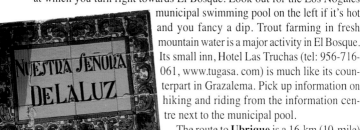

municipal swimming pool on the left if it's hot and you fancy a dip. Trout farming in fresh mountain water is a major activity in El Bosque. Its small inn, Hotel Las Truchas (tel: 956-716-061, www.tugasa. com) is much like its counterpart in Grazalema. Pick up information on hiking and riding from the information centre next to the municipal pool.

The route to **Ubrique** is a 16-km (10-mile) long mountainous road. Streams fill the Embalse de los Hurones on the right. Halfway along, you will see the ruins of the Castillo de Tavizna on the left. Many of isolated Ubrique's 18,000 population are involved in the thriving leather industry, which makes elegant leatherware and accessories for top labels. Rumour has it that some workshops attach pirate labels. *Piel de Ubrique* is good-quality leather from which factories or family workshops make well-designed products. You can watch work in progress and may be tempted by the goods on sale.

If it's time for lunch, find a place in town or stop at the **Venta el Chorizo** on the road to Cortes to sample its choice of sausages. The small, lonely

Above: view from the approach to Arcos de la Frontera

Plaza Mamelón. From here it is just one block further to the **Real Escuela Andaluza de Arte Ecuestre** (shows: Tues and Thur at noon, also Fri in August; reservations on tel: 956-318-008), where you can see one of the country's finest equestrian shows, in which the horses execute elaborate manoeuvres to music. On other days, you can visit the premises to watch rehearsals.

Shellfish Shore and Cádiz

Return to your car, and leave Jerez by the N-IV, heading for **Puerto de Santa María**. This town on the Bay of Cádiz was the main shipping port for sherry destined for South America and northern Europe. It also has a number of wine cellars, the best known of which is **Osborn**e (Mon–Fri 10.30am–1pm by appointment; tel: 956-869-100, www.osborne.es), and a castle, San Marcos, built on the site of an old Moorish mosque. But the town is most famous for its shellfish, and seafood bars line its **Ribera del Marisco** – (Shellfish Shore). Order a portion of cooked prawns, then settle at a pavement table to enjoy this delicacy with a glass of cold beer or chilled *fino* sherry.

An alternative to driving into Cádiz and finding somewhere to park is to leave your car on the quayside at Puerto de Santa María and take a boat. You have a choice: the chugging, old-fashioned *Vapor de El Puerto* is more romantic, while the catamaran is faster, cheaper and more frequent. Both leave from terminals on the bank of the Rio Guadalete, a few steps from Ribera del Marisco.

Otherwise, return to your car and follow signs to **Cádiz**. A modern bridge takes you over the Bay of Cádiz to the city, which stands on a narrow isthmus, almost completely surrounded by sea. Turn right, and drive through the unappealing modern section until you reach the entrance to the old town, the **Puerta de Tierra**. Its enormous stone walls indicate the defences needed by a port city that was a tempting prize for foreign invaders.

In 1587 a fleet commanded by Sir Francis Drake attacked the growing Spanish armada as it lay peacefully at anchor in the bay, before sacking the city, spreading terror up and down the coast and making off with 3,000 barrels of sherry. In less than three months during that summer, Drake's fleet captured or sank 60 Spanish fishing vessels and 40 coasters laden with materials that were intended to supply the Spanish navy. The incident was triumphantly celebrated in Elizabethan England and became known as 'the singeing of the king of Spain's beard'.

Bear left and park on the promenade, Campo del Sur. Then follow the signs to the Ayuntamiento on Plaza San Juan de Dios, and pick up a map at the tourist office there. The old part of the city is compact enough to be

Left: the Mirador Torre de Poniente, Cadiz's cathedral. **Above:** a world-beating sherry. **Right:** the bullring at Puerto de Santa María

explored on foot. For your first stop, head up Calle Pelota to the Plaza de la Catedral to see Cádiz's domed **cathedral**. Later, for a quick overview of the city, make your way along the narrow streets to the **Torre Tavira** (Jun–mid-Sept: daily 10am–8pm; till 6pm at other times). Standing at 45m (150ft), this tower is the highest point in the city, and one of more than 100 that were used by the city's merchants as lookout posts for ships in the days when trade with the Americas was booming. In the top of the tower is a camera obscura, which projects a 360-degree view of the exterior onto a screen in a darkened room.

From the Torre Tavira, walk down Calle Nicaragua to the chapel of Felipe Neri. This is where the first Spanish constitution was signed in 1812. Then turn right along Calle San José to Plaza de la Mina, and the **Museo de Cádiz** (Tues 2.30–8.30pm, Wed–Sat 9am–8.30pm, Sun 9am– 2.30pm). The museum devotes space to archaeology and to art. The most fascinating exhibits are the Phoenician sarcophagi that were discovered in this region. The Phoenicians, seafaring traders from present-day Lebanon, are said to have founded a trading post in Cádiz in 1,000BC, which suggests that Cádiz is the oldest continuously inhabited city in Europe.

18. LA AXARQUIA REGION, NERJA AND FRIGILIANA
(see map, p50)

The coast east of Málaga is much less developed than the strip to the west. The main resort is Nerja, with spectacular caves nearby. Inland is the beautiful upland area of La Axarquia, with pretty villages to explore.

The coast this side of Málaga was developed later than the environs of Marbella, and caters for Spanish and foreign families who want a quiet, cheap seaside holiday on the Costa del Sol. Fields of sugar cane, first introduced by the Moors, cover much of the flatlands. And so does plastic, under which vegetable and salad crops are grown.

Nerja has seen spectacular growth and it has not all been well controlled. Drive into the town and follow the signs to the **Balcón de Europa** – there's a car park nearby. King Alfonso XII declared this promontory to be the balcony of Europe when he visited the town in 1885 during a tour of the south coast to commiserate with the local people in the aftermath of an earthquake. The south coast lies along a geological fault line, but, much like Californians who live with a similar problem, local peo-

Above: a gate in the stone walls that protected Cádiz from invaders

ple don't worry much about it. Take in the views and have some refreshments at an outdoor café.

You can't help but notice the British accents, as Nerja is very much a British enclave, and has been for many years. The town has some good shops, especially along calles Almirante Ferrándiz and Pintada. Surviving among the commercialism are old houses, whose heavy doorways hide plant-filled patios. Along these streets and those connecting them is an international collection of bars and eateries. Attractive beaches lie below the cliffs, small coves nearest the town, and the long Playa de Burriana to the east with the Parador (state-owned hotel) sited above it.

Some 4km (2½ miles) east on the N340, just past the aqueduct, are the **Cuevas de Nerja** (summer: daily 10am–2pm, 4–8pm; winter: 10am–2pm, 4–6.30pm). These caves, which are among the most spectacular in Spain, were discovered in 1959 by some boys in search of bats. Since then archaeologists have found evidence that Cro-Magnon man inhabited them some 20,000 years ago. Evidence of the Roman settlement of Detunda appears in the intensively worked patchwork of terraced plots stepping down to the sea around this delightfully unspoilt hamlet. From its *balcón* you can see the dramatic coastline of Granada province where mountains drop sharply to the sea. Return to the outskirts of Nerja and follow signs to Frigiliana.

The Fight Against Felipe II

Frigiliana appears as a white splash against the greyish lower folds of the Sierra Tejeda. Terraces of vegetables, vines and fruit trees lie below. Park at the village entrance near the old sugar factory and walk left up to the old part, where dazzling white buildings line stepped streets. Ceramic tiles tell the tale of the village's valiant fight against Felipe II's troops in the Moorish rebellion of 1569. The **Garden Bar** (Wed–Mon; tel: 952-533-185) above the town has a barbecue and bistro menu that often features succulent roast lamb, served under thatched parasols. Alternatively, for some tasty local food, try **La Bodeguilla** (tel: 952-533-428) by the church.

A number of shops sell craft items and Frigiliana's strong and tasty *vino del terreno*, which is typical of the Axarquía's small-scale production. The whitewashed beds you see near local *cortijos* (farm estates) are for sun-drying the moscatel grapes for raisins and wines with a high sugar content. The village is also famous for its *miel de caña* – cane molasses.

Take the road below the village and follow signs to **Torrox**. Take care on the 14km (8¾ miles) of this high, winding road. Olive trees and vines contrast with avocado and subtropical fruits. At Torrox go north to **Cómpeta**, 15km (9¼ miles) away through yet more attractive scenery. Cómpeta is an

Right: underground caves

attractive, wine-making town with a number of good, inexpensive restaurants, many of them with good views of the surrounding hills. The most direct way back down to the coast is via Sayalonga and Algarrobo, which will bring you to a junction with the A7 motorway. An interesting detour before you descend from the hills is to Archez and Salares, both of which have exquisite, brick church towers adapted from *mudéjar* minarets. After visiting them, follow the signs to Vélez-Málaga and then back on to the motorway west for Málaga.

19. THE COSTA TROPICAL *(see pull-out map)*

Beyond Nerja, Spain's southern coast changes character and becomes a series of headlands and bays occupied by relatively small resorts that have a more authentic Spanish flavour than those on the Costa del Sol.

Allow over two hours for the drive to the Costa Tropical from Marbella. If coming from the far side of Málaga, avoid the city ring road during the rush hour between approximately 7.30 and 9am.

From Marbella, take the N340/A7 motorway to Málaga and negotiate the ring road towards Almeria. On the other side of Málaga, the motorway is toll free, and after Rincón de la Victoria traffic usually thins out considerably. Shortly after Nerja the motorway veers away from the coast and eventually peters out. It is being extended in phases via a chain of tunnels and viaducts to join up with the one coming south from Granada and construction work is ongoing. Sooner or later you will be obliged to take the old N340 coast road, which is windy but offers the compensation of great sea views.

As soon as the headlands begin, you are officially on the 'Costa Tropical', the coast of the province of Granada, so-named because it enjoys a

micro-climate that is perfect for the cultivation of tropical fruits. The first resort you come to after Nerja is **La Herradura**, framed by a perfect scoop of bay protected by two headlands, the Punta de la Mona and Cerro Gordo. There are good places to eat on the beach, notably El Chambao de Joaquín (tel: 958-640-044) which prepares a giant paella at weekend lunchtimes.

Beneath the lighthouse on the Punta de la Mona is Marina del Este, a development of villas and apartments around a delightful yacht harbour. The offshore waters are renowned for their good scuba diving.

Almuñecar and Salobreña

Back on the N340, continue to **Almuñecar**, the largest resort on the Costa Tropical, which was founded by the Phoenicians and became a Roman port by the name of Sexi. The traffic system is slightly chaotic, but Almuñecar is not large and there is usually somewhere to park on the seafront, from where it is only a short walk to the few sights. The tourist office is housed in a quaint mock Arab-style villa, the Palacete la Najarra. Just up the road is the Parque del Majuelo, a small botanical garden of sub-tropical plants laid out around the ruins of a Phoenician-Roman fish salting factory. A short stiff walk up hill is the half-restored castle (10.30am–1.30pm, 4–6.30pm) that served as a holiday home for the Nazrid kings of Granada. Outside Almuñecar, there are some fine, neglected stretches of Roman aqueduct on the road towards Otivar in a lush valley of tropical orchards.

The N340 continues east, and round a few more curves is the prettiest town on this stretch of coast, **Salobreña**. As you near it you'll see the chimney of Europe's last sugar mill, which closed in 2006, bringing to an end an industry that had existed since the Arabs first planted sugar canes here in the 10th century.

Take the main turn-off into town and park where you can. The old town swarms up over a great rock: you can drive up into it but streets are narrow and parking difficult, and the best way to explore it is on foot. From the town centre walk up the steep Calle Nuestra Señora del Rosario towards an ochre-coloured fountain and the Plaza del Antiguo Mercado. A flight of steps to the right leads to the Museo Histórico on the Plaza del Ayuntamiento. Just off here is the church of Nuestra Señora del Rosario and a curious medieval vaulted tunnel over a street, La Boveda. Continue uphill and you'll find yourself on cobbled Calle Andrés Segovia, which brings you to Salobreña's restored Arab castle, a pleasant enclosure with good views all around. The views are almost as good from the rooftop terrace of the nearby **Pesetas** restaurant (tel: 958-610-182) next to the church.

Head down hill from the castle and the church to the sea. Salobreña's two pebbly beaches are pleasant places to walk as they are not too built up. They are separated by a conspicuous rock, El Peñon, on which stands a restaurant of the same name (tel: 958-610-538) with a relaxing, cane-shaded terrace hanging over the water. In summer, fish and octopus are grilled on spits on the sand.

If you want to make an extended trip and include an overnight stay, head north from Salobreña to visit Granada, only 45 minutes' drive away, and return to Málaga on the inland motorway via Antequera.

Left: Salobreña

Leisure
Activities

SHOPPING

Marbella has a well-earned reputation for fancy shops with fancy prices. All of the big-name fashion houses are represented, both in the main town and, especially, in Puerto Banús. This is the place to look for high fashion, leather goods and jewellery.

For one-stop shopping that incorporates everything from food and wine to clothes, books, music, appliances, sports accessories and souvenirs, Marbella has two large complexes. The **Costa Marbella** centre near Puerto Banús is part of El Corte Inglés, Spain's largest department-store chain. The large Hipercor supermarket is located on the ground floor, while other departments are on the two upper floors. North of the town, on the Ojén road, is the **La Cañada** shopping mall, which has a large supermarket, Al Campo, and a large number of boutiques, speciality shops and fast-food outlets. This is the place to look for bargains in Marbella.

The shops in Málaga *(Itinerary 3)* are generally cheaper, and there is a wide choice of goods at the El Corte Inglés department store, and in the speciality shops and boutiques in the calle Marqués de Larios area. Torremolinos, which is especially appealing to younger tastes, and Fuengirola also offer a good and varied choice of shops, and both have a less exclusive image, and generally lower prices than you'll find in Marbella. Nerja *(Itinerary 18)*, east of Málaga, is another resort town with a fair selection of quality outlets, and the choice is increasing in Estepona *(Itinerary 9)* especially for arts and crafts.

Inland, too, you should be on the lookout for interesting shops, especially if you want to buy souvenirs that represent local arts and crafts. Some of the best bargains are to be found in Ronda (antiques, boots and shoes), Grazalema (blankets), Ubrique (leather accessories), Frigiliana (ceramics, basket work) and Cómpeta (ceramics).

In Gibraltar, Main Street at one time formed

a shopping emporium that was especially popular with British expats on the Costa del Sol who yearned for imported goods such as tea, horseradish sauce and Colman's mustard. The colony's tax-free status made it an attractive place to buy electronic gadgets and photographic equipment. Most imported food items are now available in shops on the Costa del Sol, and the price difference for hi-fi and camera equipment is no longer that great, so the Rock has lost some of its allure as a shopper's paradise. There are still good buys, however, in cigarettes and spirits.

Marbella's Main Shopping Areas

There are shopping areas throughout Marbella: in the Old Town, on Avenida Ramón y Cajal, at the Marbella Centre at the avenue's eastern end; along Avenida Miguel Cano and the streets west of it, including Calle Alonso Bazán; on the whole stretch of Avenida Ricardo Soriano; in Puerto Banús, including the nearby Cristamar and Costa Marbella complexes; in Nueva Andalucía's Centro Plaza, and along San Pedro's main street.

Small arcades in some of the top hotels have boutiques with a select range, mostly high-fashion clothing and accessories. There are also shops that are especially good for home-decoration items in the commercial centres that line the coastal highway.

Outdoor Markets

Mercadillos (weekly outdoor markets, 9am– 2pm) are a great place for bargains. Even if you don't buy anything, a roam around the stalls gives a colourful insight into Andalusian life. *Mercadillo* prices are unbeatable. A copy of a designer cotton shirt might go for around 15 euros; a pair of blue jeans for half the price of those sold by department stores. The same goes for shoes, towels, blankets and sheets, perfumes and toiletries, and ceramics and cooking ware. And, of course, markets have the freshest seasonal fruit and vegetables.

Left: embracing the stereotype

The Marbella *mercadillo*, in the fairground east of the town centre, is open on Monday; its counterpart in San Pedro operates on Thursdays, on the Calle Jorge Guillén. The Nueva Andalucía art and antiques market near the bullring opens on Saturdays. The Sunday *mercadillo* in Puerto de Estepona is good for arts and crafts. The biggest outdoor market on the Málaga coast is held in Fuengirola's fairground on Tuesdays. On Saturdays the flea market at the same place has hundreds of stalls selling an incredible assortment of second-hand items.

What to Buy
Antiques
Silver and gold work, religious paintings and statues, carved and gilt picture frames, ceramic tiles, pitchers and washing bowls, handmade glass, embossed copperware, fine lace, embroidered cloth, and inlaid and rustic furniture are among the things to buy.

The big emporium at El Rastro de Río Verde (N340 km176) is a good place to find bargains. In the centre of Marbella, scout around El Arte de Giles and Calle Jacinto Benavente. There's an outdoor antiques market on Saturday morning near the bullring in Nueva Andalucía. Better buys are often found in hole-in-the-wall shops in inland villages and towns, and also in the weekly *mercadillos*, where stallholders may not be aware of the value of something they are trying to sell.

Ronda is one of the main antiques centres in Andalucía, especially when it comes to furniture. Often though, the furniture is not genuinely antique, but rather a new creation made with old, seasoned wood. These might be fine pieces, but bear the lack of authenticity in mind when haggling over the price.

Art
Marbella's galleries don't have much art of the type worth investing in for strictly financial reasons – unless you're lucky enough to find an exhibition of works for sale by Antonio Lopez, Antoni Tàpies, Miquel Barceló or other names among the country's *firmas consagradas* ('hallowed signatures'). But southern Spain has attracted an enormous number of serious, dedicated artists, both Spanish and foreign, and there is a lot of good art to be seen on permanent exhibition and at special showings.

Recommended galleries include: Fabien Fryn's (Marbella Club, Bulevar Príncipe Alfonso de Hohenlohe), Messeg Design, Calle Aluminio 6, Marbella, El Catalejo (Urbanización Marbella Real) and Sammer Gallery, which has two branches in Puerto Banus. The serious collector will probably want to explore Málaga's galleries.

Crafts
When it comes to buying gifts and souvenirs, ceramics top the list of many visitors to the region. There are traditional utilitarian and decorative items and imaginative new shapes and designs. They are roughly or finely formed, glazed or unglazed, in bright colours or finely

food and wine shops

71

painted. Some of the best known of Andalucía's ceramics, readily available from shops on the Costa del Sol, are the blue-, green- and white-glazed ceramics from Granada, and the green ceramics from Ubeda in Jaén. Pieces range from souvenir ashtrays and vases to complete china dinner services from a renowned factory in Seville. Then of course there are the unavoidable Lladró porcelain figurines from Valencia, which are much sought-after by enthusiasts throughout the world. Ceramic shops are everywhere, and don't forget to check for bargains at the outdoor markets, where there is also plenty of choice.

Designer items for home decoration by Spain's new wave of creative talent can be found in many different media, from papier-mâché to glass and metals. These can make great gifts, as can goods woven from esparto or wicker. Baskets, whether for decoration or daily use, come in all shapes and sizes. Other articles include table mats, lampshades, painted wall hangings, picture frames, slippers, and all manner of decorated boxes.

There was a time when leather items were considerably cheaper in Spain than in other European countries, but this is no longer the case. Still, it is worth looking for small workshops that sell handcrafted items made to their own design. The best buys of a range of leather goods can be made directly from the leather factories in Ubrique. And don't forget to check the shoe stores on the coast for shoes and Spanish boots.

You might want to purchase some traditional fiesta dress accessories, as sported by Andalusian women. These include fans, *mantillas* (lace or silk shawls worn over the head and shoulders), and decorative combs. Numerous visitors buy such items as mementos or gifts. Be warned that there is a great variation in quality. The best buys are not usually found in souvenir shops but in speciality shops used by local women.

Clothing

Clothes of comparable quality cost more in Spain (especially in Marbella) than in the United States and in other part of Europe. Children's clothing in particular is extremely expensive due to the Spanish predilection for dressing children in the finest apparel.

It is nevertheless well worth browsing the fashion boutiques of Marbella. Here you will find shops with international names such as Gucci and Benetton, but for fashionable threads, jewellery and other accessories it is perhaps best to go for the labels from the big crop of talented Spanish designers who have risen to prominence in the past decade. These include Adolfo Dominguez, Jesús del Pozo, Manuel Piña, Sybilla, Purificación Garcia, Roser Mercé, José Tomas, Toni Miró, Pedro Moreno and Vitorio y Luchino. Check out the outlets of the Spanish chain Zara for good fashion at reasonable prices.

Music

You may want to buy a classical Spanish guitar or a small flamenco model. A custom-made *guitarra española* costs a fortune; cheaper factory-made guitars produce a fine enough sound. A pair of castanets also make a fine memento. A recommended outlet for musical instruments in Marbella is La Música on Avenida Severo Ochoa 47.

There's a good selection of Spanish sounds at the Disco 2000 shop on Avenida Ramón y Cajal 20 in central Marbella, and also at the Costa Marbella shopping centre. Here you'll find flamenco, Spanish pop and *zarzuela*, as Spanish light opera is known.

Food and Wine

The Hipercor supermarket in the Costa Marbella shopping centre near Puerto Banús is the best place for gifts and mementos of the edible kind. You might not manage a whole cured *jamón serrano* ham, but there are many more portable typically Spanish packaged foods. These include a variety of olives, capers, sherry vinegar, saffron, paprika, sausages, raisins and dried figs.

Spanish wine – sherries, sweet wine from Málaga, aged reds from Rioja and Ribera del Duero, whites from Rueda and Rias Baixas, and sparkling *cava* – are all great value. Spanish brandy is also a good buy. Casa Pablo in central Marbella (Gomez de la Serna 2) is a good place to look. The Hipercor supermarket also has a big selection; its house brands (sold under the name of the vineyard's region) are good value. Check out your country's customs regulations before packing alcohol or other liquids, however.

Left: blue-and-white pottery, a local favourite

EATING OUT

Enjoying fine food in relaxing surroundings is one of the great pleasures of visiting the Costa del Sol. Marbella in particular has a wide choice of restaurants, from cheap and cheerful beachside establishments to stylish restaurants that serve wonderfully prepared and presented cuisine. Aside from Spain's new generation of chefs, a number of chefs have come from elsewhere in Europe to ply their trade, thereby adding to the gastronomic variety. Cooks in Andalucía have at their disposal fine raw ingredients, whether it's fresh fruit and vegetables, fish and shellfish, or pork and lamb. The quality of the beef, which used to be poor, has improved considerably.

What to Order

Traditional Andalusian cuisine tends to present its ingredients as simply as possible. *Gazpacho* is a tasty liquid blend of tomatoes, peppers, garlic, oil, vinegar and (possibly stale) bread served up as a refreshing cold soup. A Málaga variation is *ajo blanco*, a cold soup made with fresh almonds and garlic and garnished with grapes.

Seafood is a recurring ingredient in many soups and in stews such as *zarzuela de mariscos*, but is usually eaten either plainly grilled or *a la sal* – baked in a crust of salt. The local speciality is fried fish – anchovies, squid, hake, baby sole – whose quality depends on the freshness of the fish and the

standard of the oil. Ask for *fritura Malagueña* if you want to try a platter of assorted fried fish.

Renewed interest in Andalucía's Moorish history has seen the triumphant return of such recipes as lamb roasted with honey. Regional specialities from elsewhere in Spain, particularly the Basque country, are also represented on Costa del Sol menus.

Paella, the national dish, originated in Valencia. Saffron-flavoured rice is garnished with diced fish, shellfish, chicken and pork, plus vegetables, cooked and served in the traditional paella pan. Although there are some places on the coast that cook it well, the paella served in most tourist restaurants is frequently a formless yellow goo that does little justice to the genuine article.

A Spanish winter speciality is *cocido*, a hotpot consisting of ingredients all cooked together – meat, chicken, ham bone, sausages, vegetables, dried beans and lentils, potatoes – to make two courses: a soup with rice or noodles, then the meat and vegetables.

Tapas

It has long been a tradition in Spanish bars to serve small portions of food with each drink. The idea originated with the custom of covering glasses with a small lid or plate (*tapa*). Eventually someone thought to put titbits of food on these plates, perhaps to help the customers soak up the alcohol. *Tapas* were originally served free; they still

Above: popular cafe in Tarifa

are in some parts of Andalucía, but alas not on the Costa del Sol. In fact, be aware that the price of *tapas* can easily add up to more than the cost of a set menu. *Tapas* are usually displayed under glass with prices indicated on a blackboard, so they are easy to order even if you don't speak Spanish.

A *tapa* can be as simple as a few olives, a wafer of cheese, a dollop of salad or a few marinated anchovies. One of the best choices is a slice or two of *Serrano* ham, which is salt-cured and dried in the mountain air. The best – and, at three or four times the price of other cured hams, the dearest – comes from Jabugo in the mountains of Huelva province, where it is made from free-range Ibérico pigs, which are fed on acorns.

Cooked combinations, usually served hot, display the most inventiveness. You might try kidneys in sherry sauce; octopus diced with tomato and garlic; rabbit in almond sauce; lamb stew; crisply fried fish; prawns; mussels and other shellfish (plain or with sauce); salty fried aubergines.

Wine

Spain has more land devoted to vineyards than any other country, and the quality of the wines has improved beyond recognition. Prices have increased, but Spanish wines are nevertheless excellent value for money.

Start your meal with an aperitif of chilled, dry sherry *fino*. Sherries from Jerez have long been the most important Spanish wines in terms of international prestige and exports. Córdoba's Montilla-Moriles region produces *vinos generosos* (wines with a high alcohol content) that are similar to sherry. Both these regions produce white table wines, including Castillo de San Diego from Barbadillo in Sanlúcar de Barrameda (Cádiz), which is one of Spain's best-selling whites.

Andalusian whites tend to be on the thin side; though very refreshing they are not strong on character. The best Spanish whites are Verdejo wines from Rueda and Albariño from Rías Baixas in Galicia. The country's wineries are currently doing some nifty things with French white grapes such as chardonnay and sauvignon blanc.

You can buy both young and aged reds (classified as *crianza*, *reserva* or *gran reserva*, depending on the time spent in the cask). Some of the best are made from Spain's tempranillo grape. Look for reds from Rioja, Ribera del Duero and Somontano. Lighter reds from the La Mancha and Valdepeñas regions have less structure and character, but are suitable as a light summer accompaniment to a meal. Spaniards often like to mix this type of wine with lemonade to make a refreshing *tinto de verano* ('summer red wine'). To end a meal, try one of Málaga's famous sweet, heavy dessert wines. Look out too for aged sweet Pedro Ximenez wines from the Montilla-Moriles region. Villages throughout Andalucía produce their own *vino del terreno* for local consumption. This usually packs quite a kick, so sample with caution. You'll find it in villages such as Manilva, Cómpeta and Frigiliana.

Hours, Etiquette and Tipping

Spain is famous for its late dining hours. However, due to the annual influx of tourists, restaurant hours on the Costa del Sol tend to be more in line with the rest of Europe. Lunch starts at any time between 1 and 3pm, while dinner commences at around 9pm.

To be safe, always phone ahead to book a table, especially at the better restaurants. Casual (but not scruffy) dress is acceptable at most establishments, as are children. You should be a bit smarter at the more expensive places, particularly for dinner.

Although service is included in the restaurant bill, it is traditional to tip the waiter around 5–10 percent. If you are paying with a credit card, it is best to tip in cash.

Price guide per head for a three course meal with house wine:
€€€ = over €36
€€ = €18–€36
€ = Under €18

Marbella

Altamirano
Plaza Altamirano 3
Tel: 952-824-932
Located in the Old Town, this is a highly popular establishment that serves excellent seafood at good prices. €€

Antonio
Muelle Ribera, Puerto Banús
Tel: 952-814-536

A Puerto Banús institution, specialising in seafood – particularly paella. €€€

Casa Nostra
Calle Camino José Cela 12
Tel: 952-861-108
Popular and well-run Italian restaurant. €

Cipriano
Avenida Playas del Duque, Puerto Banús
Tel: 952-811-077
Near the Puerto Banús harbour, one of the best places in the area for fresh seafood. €€

Don Leone
Muelle Ribera 45, Puerto Banús
Tel: 952-814-962
Fresh pasta and other Italian favourites on a summer terrace, by the wharf. €€

El Portalon
Carretera de Cádiz–Málaga km178
Tel: 952-827-880
Across the street from the Marbella Club, this restaurant successfully combines the atmosphere and flavours of Castile with original creative cuisine. €€€

El Puente Romano
Hotel Puente Romano
Carretera de Cádiz km177
Tel: 952-820-900
Especially recommended for summer dining on a terrace. Imaginative options plus Spanish and international favourites. €€€

In Vino
Carretera Almeria–Cádiz, Marbella
Tel: 952-771-211
Fine wine in a stylish setting. Especially pleasant when you can eat on the terrace. Closed Tues; dinner only in summer. €€€

La Meridiana
Camino de la Cruz s/n
Tel: 952-776-90
Strikingly imaginative cuisine in a stunning modern palace. Dinner only in summer. €€€

La Pesquera
Plaza de la Victoria
Tel: 952-765-170
Informal bar/restaurant with a wide selec-tion of seafood and grilled meats. Several other branches in and around Marbella. €

Marbella Club Grill
Bulevar Príncipe Alfonso de Hohenlohe
Tel: 952-822-211
Fine dining in Marbella's original hotel. €€€

Red Pepper
Muelle Ribera, Puerto Banús
Tel: 952-812-148
A lively Greek taverna on the front line. €€

Santiago
Paseo Marítimo
Tel: 952-770-078
Fish and seafood restaurant with an excellent reputation. €€

Toni Dalli
Carretera de Cádiz km176
Tel: 952-770-035
A Marbella institution serving good Italian food and run by former tenor Toni Dalli, who sometimes sings for your supper. Live music most nights. Dinner only. €€€

ZoZöi
Plaza Altamirano 1
Tel: 952-858-868
Creative international cuisine in an atmospheric setting in an old converted house. Dinner only. Closed Sun. €€€

West of Marbella

Iñaki Martínez
Pasaje de Torremolinos 3
San Pedro de Alcántara
Tel: 952-788-865
Traditional dishes cooked by a top Basque chef. Closed Sun. €€

La Rada
Avenida España, Estepona
Tel: 952-791-036
Serves fresh fish in an informal atmosphere. Closed Wed. €

Yanx
Centro Plaza, Nueva Andalucía
Tel: 952-818-861
Café with bagels, Tex-Mex and burgers. €€

eating out

Cádiz Province

Brasserie Vaca Loca
Calle Cervantes 6, Tarifa
Tel: 605-281-791
A restaurant in an enclosed pedestrianised square, specialising in barbecued kebabs, with a vegetarian option available. €€

La Palmosa
A381 Motorway, Alcalá de los Gazules
Tel: 956-413-364
There are few places to stop on the motorway between Jerez and Algeciras so this hotel-restaurant is worth knowing about. It has several dining rooms and a long bar serving a rich selection of *tapas*. €

Restaurante El Faro
Calle San Felix 15, Cádiz
Tel: 956-211-068
One of the city's best-known restaurants. An elegant place, but you can always have the day's set menu or *tapas* at the bar. €€€

Romerijo
Ribera del Marisco, Puerto de Santa María
Tel: 956-541-254
A family-run chain of shellfish shops and bars on the 'Shellfish Shore'. €€

East of Marbella

El Balandro
Paseo Marítimo, Rey de España 139
Fuengirola
Tel: 952-661-417
Specialises in grilled red meat and roast suckling pig. €€

Frutos
Urbanización Los Alamos
Ctra. de Cádiz km 228, Torremolinos
Tel: 952-381-450
This is a long-time favourite of many Malagueños. No dinner on Sunday. €€

El Higuerón
Carretera Benalmádena–Mijas
Tel: 952-119-163
Located between Fuengirola and Torremolinos and housed in a 150-year-old inn, this place serves large helpings of Spanish specialities. €€

Le Chene Liège
Urbaniación La Mairena, Ojén
Tel: 952-852-050
A 10-minute drive into the hills to the east of Marbella is rewarded by splendid views and excellent French cuisine. Dinner only. €€€

La Hacienda Paul Schiff
Urbanización Hacienda Las Chapas
Tel: 952-831-267
Long-established culinary landmark housed in a pleasant villa. Creative Spanish and international dishes. Closed Mon, Tues, except in Aug; dinner only in summer. €€€

La Langosta
Francisco Cano 1, Fuengirola
Tel: 952-475-049
Long-established eatery specialising in lobster dishes. Closed Sun; dinner only. €€

Portofino
Paseo Marítimo 29, Fuengirola
Tel: 952-470-643
Italian, Spanish and international dishes. Closed Mon; dinner only in summer. €€

Ventorrillo de la Perra
Avenida de Benalmádena 85
Arroyo de la Miel
Tel: 952-441-966
Near Torremolinos, an 18th-century inn that serves local food and international dishes. Closed Mon. €€

Right: churros, popular for breakfast

Inland from Marbella

Refugio del Juanar
Sierra Blanca, Ojén
Tel: 952-881-000
A former hunting lodge surrounded by pine trees in the hinterland behind Marbella. Game dishes in season. €€

Taberna del Alabardero
Carretera Ronda km167
Tel: 952-812-794
Part of a chain run by a priest, the Taberna specialises in Basque cuisine. €€€

Málaga

Antonio Martín
Plaza de la Malagueta
Tel: 952-227-398
Late 19th century. A good place to try *fritura Malagueña* (assorted fried fish). €€

Café de París
Velez Málaga 8
Tel: 952-225-043
Creative cuisine. Closed Mon. €€€

Chinitas
Moreno Monroy 4
Tel: 952-210-972
Classic regional cuisine. €€

Parador de Gibralfaro
Castillo de Gibralfaro
Tel: 952-221-902
Fine Spanish and international cuisine and unbeatable views over the bay. €€

Ronda

Hotel Don Miguel
Plaza de España 4
Tel: 952-877-722
Traditional Spanish food and views of Ronda's Puente Viejo bridge. €€

Parador de Ronda
Plaza de España
Tel: 952-877-500
Local, regional and international dishes. €€€

Pedro Romero
Virgen de la Paz 18
Tel: 952-871-110

Good *Rabo de toro* (braised bull's tail). €€

Tragabuches
Calle José Aparicio 1
Tel: 952-404-200
Innovative renditions of classic Andalusian dishes. Closed Sun evening and Mon. €€€

Antequera

El Angelote
Plaza Coso Viejo
Tel: 952-703-465
Andalusian cuisine. Closed Mon. €€

Hotel Lozano
Avenida Principal 2, Poligono Industrial
Tel: 952-842-712
Good food at reasonable prices. €€

Parador de Antequera
Garcia del Olmo
Tel: 952-840-261
Great views over the Antequera valley. €€

Nerja

Casa Luque
Plaza Cavana 2
Tel: 952-521-004
A taste of northern Spain. Closed Wed. €€€

Pepe Rico
Almirante Ferrandiz 28
Tel: 952-520-247
Spanish and Italian inspired food. €€

Above: plenty of bars offer live music or club nights

NIGHTLIFE

Clubs

Marbella's famed nightlife revolves around its many bars and clubs. An evening out can consist of a round of *tapas* taverns in the old part of Marbella, or dancing to music at one of the trendy bars that are so plentiful in the country's most hedonistic resort.

If you're looking for nightlife hot spots, Puerto Banús is the place to be. People meet at bars such as Sinatra or Salduba, at the entrance to the harbour, to decide on their next move. Nightlife venues go in and out of fashion from one season to the next. Marbella is quite fickle in this respect, but some of the steady favourites include La Comedia, News Café, Old Joy's Pub and The Navy Club.

If you're after something more sedate or sophisticated, head inland from Puerto Banús and sample the scene at la Notte (tel: 952-776-190), a piano bar that adjoins La Meridina restaurant.

The most renowned and long-lasting disco scene is at the exclusive Olivia Valere club (tel: 952-828-861) on Carretera de Istán, which is popular with film stars and sheikhs. Somewhat more casual are Bohemian and Tibu, both in Plaza Antonio Banderas, in Puerto Banús.

During the summer months much of the action shifts to Marbella's beach clubs, such as the Babaloo Beach. Many organise regular theme parties at which revellers dance the night away. One of the more exclusive beachside venues is the Suite del Mar, in the Hotel Puente Romano.

Further along the coast you will find exciting nightlife centres at the Puerto de Benalmádena marina and in Torremolinos, where there is an active gay scene.

Many of the bars in Puerto Banús and Marbella feature live music some days of the week, as do a handful of clubs in Málaga. In summer there are concerts and theatre performances at the auditorium in the Parque de la Constitución in central Marbella, and at several other venues around town. However, internationally known acts tend to appear in Málaga, at the city's Teatro Cervantes (tel: 952-224-100) or, when it comes to major rock concerts, the Málaga bullring.

Flamenco

Though the roots of flamenco are found in Moorish songs, the tradition was adopted by Spanish gypsies as the musical expression of an impoverished and often oppressed race. The pinnacle of the true flamenco singer's art is the body of great songs known as *cante jondo* (deep song). In its multitude of variants, *cante jondo* features wailing lyrics that speak of passion and suffering, to the accompaniment of a guitar and rhythmic clapping.

Pure *cante jondo* is a minority art that is inaccessible even to most Spaniards. At its best, it is seen in the private *peñas* (flamenco clubs, the most famous of which are in Jerez), or in the summer flamenco festivals held in villages of the Andalusian hinterland.

The *tablaos* (flamenco shows) on the Costa del Sol present a diluted version that focuses on the lighter, more flowery form of flamenco. Although purists frown on these spectacles as travesties of the real thing, for a rollicking show of boisterous singing, clapping, and thunderous foot-stomping dances, an evening at one of the flamenco clubs on the coast can be a lot of fun. It will also give you an insight into this uniquely Andalusian art form.

Flamenco Ana María
Plaza de Santo Cristo 4–5
Marbella
Tel: 952-860-704
The traditional Marbella venue for flamenco shows. The curtain rises at around 11pm.

Bona Dea
Carretera Almería–Cádiz km 168
Estepona
Tel: 952-880-435
Bona Dea offers a flamenco spectacle with gourmet dinner. Dinner is from 9pm, and the show starts at 11pm.

Taberna Flamenca Pepe Lopez
Tel: 952-381-284
Located on Torremolinos's Plaza de la Gamba Alegre, this is one of several long-established flamenco clubs on the coast.

Casinos
Formal dress and possession of a passport or other form of identification are required to gain access to the coast's gambling casinos. All offer roulette, blackjack and other table games, plus slot machines.

Casino Marbella
Hotel Nueva Andalucía
Nueva Andalucía, Marbella
Tel: 952-814-000
Slot machines available from 4pm, gaming room from 8pm.

Casino Torrequebrada
Avenida del Sol
Benalmádena–Costa
Tel: 952-446-000
Gaming rooms open at 9pm. Live show in the Fortuna Nightclub starts at 10.30pm.

Casino de San Roque
Carretera N340 km127, San Roque
Tel: 965-780-100
The coast's newest casino, past Sotogrande. Gaming room opens at 8pm.

Cinema
Complejo Cinematográfico,
Gran Marbella
Muelle Ribera, Puerto Banús
Tel: 952-816-421
A modern complex with eight theatres, one of which screens recent releases in English.

Attractions
Escuela de Arte Ecuestre
N340 km159, Estepona
Tel: 952-808-077
Horse centre, with dressage shows.

Garden of Eagles
(Centro de Aves Rapaces)
Monte Calamorro, Benalmádena
Tel: 952-568-239
Birds of prey show and falconry display.

Hipódromo Costa del Sol
Urbanización El Chaparral, Mijas–Costa
Tel: 952-592-700
To the west of Fuengirola, the coast's horse-racing track stages regular races during winter, and occasional evening races in summer.

Sealife
Dársena de Levante, Benalmádena–Costa
Tel: 952-560-150
An aquariumn located in the Benalmádena sports harbour. Features a variety of fish life, the highlight being a large shark tank.

Selwo
N340 km162.5, Loma del Monte
Estepona
Tel: 952-792-150
A 100-hectare (250-acre) wildlife park with lions, tigers, elephants, giraffes and many more wild species.

Tivoli World
Arroyo de la Miel
Tel: 952-257-016
Amusement park with over two dozen rides, regular shows, several restaurants and bars.

Left: flamenco dancing

CALENDAR OF EVENTS

The local calendar is dotted with *fiestas*, *ferias* and *romerías*. A *fiesta* often celebrates a saint's day or a similar religious event; the previous night features music and dancing. Floats form a procession through the streets and there is frequently an open-air Mass. *Ferias* are week-long communal parties. *Romerías* are pilgrimages to a religious shrine in the country.

A number of shops and restaurants close in August, when most of Spain is on holiday.

January

Cabalgata de los Reyes (5–6th): float parades; the Three Wise Men disperse sweets to the crowds, and distribute gifts to children. Saints feast days – St Anthony in Mijas and Nerja, St Sebastián in Casabermeja.

February

Carnaval: pre-Lent outburst of indulgence.

March / April

Semana Santa (Holy Week: sees Spain return to the Dark Ages. Images of the Virgin and Christ are carried on richly ornate *pasos* (floats) by members of various brotherhoods. Hooded *penitentes*, some with feet in chains, walk ahead. Only shuffling feet, tinkling bells, banging drums and the occasional *saeta* (devotional song) break the silence; thousands of candles light the darkness. Each village and town has its own procession. It is worth making a trip to Seville for the *Feria de Abril* (starting two weeks after Easter), for the country's most exuberant spring festival.

May

Cruces de Mayo (3rd): neighbourhoods in some towns compete to form the best procession with crosses decorated with paper flowers. Children re-enact *Semana Santa* (holy week).
Corpus Christi (sometimes in June) sees more processions along streets covered with petals and sweet-smelling herbs.

June

Fiesta de San Bernabé: (week of the 11th): Processions in Marbella mark the town's conquest by the Catholic monarchs.

Noche de San Juan (23rd): celebrations involve bonfires and effigies of Judas burned at the stake. There are also some lively (and noisy) fireworks displays.

July

Virgen del Carmen (16th): honours the patroness of fishermen with boat processions. Events in Estepona, Fuengirola, Málaga and Nerja are among the biggest in the country.

August

Feria de Málaga: celebrated during the first fortnight, emulates Seville's Spring Fair.

September

Feria y Fiesta de Pedro Romero (first fortnight): features, in addition to the usual party atmosphere, major bullfighting events that include the *Corrida Goyesca* (Goyaesque Bullfight) in early 19th-century costumes.

October

Feria y Romería del Rosario. In the first full week, Fuengirola has a big *feria* and a *romería* to a field off the N340, where a model of the Virgin's shrine is installed.
Saint's Day in San Pedro de Alcántara (19th): is celebrated with an open-air Mass and a procession.

December

Folk Music Festival (28th): Traditional Malaga musicians compete in a contest at the Venta de San Cayetano, Puerto de la Torre.

Above: pretty backstreet

Practical
Information

TRAVEL ESSENTIALS

Orientation

The Costa del Sol is the coastline of Málaga province – one of Andalucía's eight provinces. Andalucía, one of Spain's 17 autonomous communities, has Seville as its capital.

Málaga city, the provincial capital, has around 500,000 inhabitants. The N340 or A7/E15 coastal highway, mostly dual carriageway, runs west from Málaga for 56km (35 miles) to Marbella, passing Málaga airport 7km (4 miles) from the city centre. There is an alternative toll motorwaý (AP7) in three parts, one going to Seville (220km/137 miles northwest of Málaga); one to Córdoba (185km/115 miles north); the third to Granada (130km/81 miles to the northeast).

When it comes to the clock, Spain is in line with the majority of European countries: in summer it is two hours ahead of GMT; in winter, one hour ahead.

Andalusians speak Spanish, although with a strong local accent that may be difficult to understand at first if you are used to hearing Spanish spoken in other parts of the country.

Climate and Clothing

The climate on the Costa del Sol is typically Mediterranean – summers are hot, winters (when most of what rain there is falls) are relatively mild, and spring and autumn both have agreeable weather.

The Sierra Blanca behind Marbella gives the city a microclimate that is a little cooler than most of the south coast in summer and a little warmer in winter.

The average temperature is 18°C (64°F) and there is an annual average of 320 days of sunshine. In the summer temperatures may exceed 30°C (86°F); in winter they rarely drop below 12°C (54°F). Loose-fitting cotton clothes are therefore an obvious choice for summer; add light sweaters for spring and autumn, and slightly heavier layers plus a light raincoat and maybe an umbrella in winter. The Costa del Sol is fairly fashion-conscious, but the style is casual.

When to Go

Any time of year is good for a visit to Spain's Costa del Sol. The summer season, when restaurants, hotels, discos and the like are in full swing, is from mid-June to the end of September. In winter, however, you will find bargains in both car hire and accommodation. Winter is probably the best season for golfers. Most nature-lovers will appreciate the glorious springtime display of flowers, both wild and in gardens.

GETTING THERE

By Air

Flying to Málaga airport on scheduled, budget or charter services, possibly with an accommodation package, is the most popular way of getting to the Costa del Sol. Seville, Jerez de la Frontera and Gibraltar are other points of arrival by air.

Travel agents will have the latest information on flights and package availability. Málaga has the usual facilities of a Grade 1 international airport, including excellent duty-free shopping. There is a regular bus service to Marbella. Check the current taxi fare to Marbella at the information desk before leaving the airport; take only registered taxis and agree the fare in advance. Airport switchboard: tel: 952-048-404.

By Road

Drivers head for Málaga and then Marbella along Spain's fast-improving road network. It is apparently possible to drive from Rome, Copenhagen or London without being stopped by traffic lights, which doesn't mean that there aren't Civil Guard motorcycle patrolmen around, who can administer heavy, on-the-spot fines for driving offences. For information, you should con-

Left: out on the open road

sult motoring organisations in your home country. Driving is on the right, and seatbelts are obligatory.

By Rail
Málaga is the Costa del Sol's main railway terminus (tel: 952-360-202) is in Calle Cuarteles. RENFE is the national rail operator. Travel agents can provide information about routes, times and fare schemes.

By Sea
Cruise liners regularly call at Málaga and a scheduled Trasmediterránea service connects with Barcelona and the Canary Islands.
   Marbella's three marinas are at:
   • Puerto Banús (tel: 952-909-800)
   • Puerto de Marbella (tel: 952-775-524)
   • Puerto Cabopino (tel: 952-831-975).

Documents
Citizens of EU countries require a national identity card or passport, but not a visa. Citizens of some other countries, such as the United States, Australia and many Latin American states, do not need visas for stays of up to 90 days. South African citizens need a visa. All non-EU citizens need a passport. If in doubt, check with the Spanish consulate in your country. Medical certificates are not required of people arriving from most parts of the world. National driving licences from most countries are valid.

Customs Regulations
Duty-free allowances for non-European Union travellers to Spain are: 800 cigarettes (or 200 cigars), 10 litres of alcohol, 90 litres of wine, or 20 litres of fortified wine. There is no duty-free allowance for those travelling between EU countries.
   Any amount of local or foreign currency can be imported, but if you are travelling with more than €3,000 this should be declared to customs.

Electricity
Spain uses AC at 220 volts, 50hz. Plugs have two round pins. Remember to pack a plug adapter (you can buy one at the airport before you leave) and visitors from the US will need a transformer if they are bringing 110V appliances on the trip.

MONEY MATTERS

The currency in Spain is the euro (€). Coins are issued in denominations of 1, 2, 5, 10, 20, and 50 cents and 1 and 2 euros. Notes are issued in denominations of 5, 10, 20, 50, 100, 200 and 500 euros.

   All major credit and charge cards are accepted, but Visa is the most common card. There are many ATMs, at which credit cards and some foreign-issued bank cards can be used to obtain money – as long as you remember your PIN number.

   Banks, which are plentiful, are the best places to exchange currency. They open Monday– Friday 9am–2pm, Saturday 9am–1pm (in summer banks are closed on Saturday). There are also many *cajas de cambio* (bureaux de change), which operate longer opening hours. These tend to offer a poorer rate of exchange than banks, but they often don't charge commission.

Tax
IVA, a value-added tax, applies on most goods and services at the rate of 7 percent. On goods and services that are considered luxuries, including things like car hire and camera film, this rises to 16 percent. If you have resident status in a non-EU country and want to make a purchase of more than €90, you might be eligible for exemption from IVA.

ACCOMMODATION

Hotels are officially rated from one up to five stars, though there is also a rating of five stars-plus *gran lujo*, which indicates a level of opulent luxury. *Hostales* are awarded one to three stars. *Pensiónes* have one or two stars. Officially classified tourist apartments (ATs) have one to three keys.

If you're looking for private lettings or specialist villa and apartment holiday firms, it's a good idea to consult the travel pages of newspapers in your home country for relevant advertisements before you set out.

Marbella has an exceptional range of top-rated hotels. The choice in the less expensive categories is more limited. The price codes in the following listings are based on a double room in high season.

€€€ = over €150
€€ = €60–€90
€ = €60

Marbella
Coral Beach
Carretera de Cádiz km176
Tel: 952-824-500
Fax: 952-826-257
www.hotelcoralbeach.com
Four-star accomodation ringed by palm trees, right on the beach in the heart of Marbella's Golden Mile, the Coral Beach has

two restaurants plus a beach club and health centre. 170 rooms. Open Mar–Nov. €€€

Gran Melia Don Pepe
José Melia s/n
Tel: 952-770-300
Fax: 952-779-954
www.solmelia.com
Located at the western end of the town, in close proximity to the beach, the 5-star Gran Melia Don Pepe is one of the oldest and most venerable of Marbella's hotels. In addition to being luxurious and impeccably maintained, it is one of the resort's most convenient hotels for the town centre. 202 rooms. €€€

Los Monteros
Carretera de Cadiz km187
Tel: 952-771-700
Fax: 952-823-721/952-825-846
www.monteros.com
The perfect choice for sports enthusiasts, the five-star Los Monteros includes the Río Real golf course, a tennis club with 10 courts, and five squash courts. There is a variety of water sports at La Cabane Beach Club. The actual accommodation is in rooms decorated with different regional themes within three pavilions surrounded by gardens. There is a choice of two restaurants. 177 rooms. €€€

Puente Romano
Carretera de Cadiz km177
Tel: 952-820-900
Fax: 952-775-766
www.puenteromano.com
This luxurious Moorish *pueblo*-style complex is surrounded by luxuriant trees, flowers and lawns that are tended by a small army of gardeners. Rooms are luxurious. The El Puente and La Plaza restaurants overlook the Roman bridge after which the hotel is named. There is a tennis club, two pools, and arrangements with three golf clubs. 293 rooms. €€€

Hotel El Fuerte
Avenida El Fuerte
Tel: 952-920-000
Fax: 952-824-411
www.fuertehoteles.com
Hotel El Fuerte is a pleasant, classic establishment, and, of all Marbella's numerous top-class hotels, it enjoys what is probably

Above: Marbella's sumptuous Puente Romano

the optimum central location – close to the sea at the eastern end of the Paseo Marítimo. 263 rooms. €€

Marbella Club Hotel
Bulevar Príncipe Alfonso de Hohenlohe
Marbella
Tel: 952-822-211
Fax: 952-829-884
www.marbellaclub.com
This is where the Costa del Sol started in the 1950s, and this legendary hotel still exudes the atmosphere of an exclusive club. It has stylishly appointed suites, bungalows and rooms, set in a subtropical garden. Public rooms are cosily luxurious, and there is a restaurant, beach club, two pools and a fitness centre. 126 rooms, 10 bungalows. €€€

Riu Rincón Andaluz
Carretera de Cadiz km173
Tel: 952-811-517
Fax: 952-814-180
www.riu.com
The pretty Riu Rincón Andaluz is modelled on an Andalusian *pueblo* (village), and is surrounded by luxury villas. Near the sea and close to Puerto Banús. 227 rooms. €€€

Lima
Avenida Antonio Belón 2
Tel: 952-770-500
Fax: 952-863-091
Email: limahotel@terra.es
Conveniently located in central Marbella, just one block from the Paseo Marítimo. The 2-star Lima is a comfortable choice, if somewhat old-fashioned, and is a good mid-range bet. 64 rooms. €€

Hostels
Enriqueta
Calle Los Caballeros 18
Tel: 952-827-552
Small, simple hostel in a great location near the Plaza de los Naranjos. 20 rooms. €

El Castillo
Plaza San Bernabé 2
Tel: 952-771-739
Well located next to the Old Town, El Castillo has basic, tasteful, clean rooms for a mostly young clientele. 26 rooms. €

Apartments
Jardines del Mar
Paraje Don Pepe
Tel: 952-776-000
Fax: 952-770-628
www.jardinesdelmar.es
Comfortable two-room apartments set in pleasant gardens. €€

Benabola Park Plaza
Paseo Marítimo de Benabola
Puerto Banús
Tel: 952-909-300
Fax: 952-812-846
www.parkplazasuiteshotel.com
Apartments for up to six people in the heart of the port. €€€

West of Marbella
Amanhavis
Calle Pilar 3
Benahavís
Tel: 952-856-026
Fax: 952-856-151
www.amanhavis.com

Beautiful modern Moorish fantasy palace in the delightful village of Benahavís, with just nine rooms/suites, each decorated with a different medieval theme relating to Spanish medieval history. €€€

Las Dunas
La Boladilla Baja
Carretera de Cádiz km163.5
Estepona
Tel: 952-809-400
Fax: 952-794-825
www.lasdunas@accor.com
Luxurious spa hotel with fitness centre and health programmes, located right next to the beach, about halfway between Estepona and Marbella. 73 rooms and 33 apartments. €€€

Kempinski
Playa El Padrón
Carretera de Cadiz km159, Estepona
Tel: 952-809-500
Fax: 952-809-550
www.kempinski-spain.com
Deluxe resort on the beach a few miles east of Estepona town centre. Four pools (one indoor) and a fitness centre. 149 rooms. €€€

El Paraíso
Urbanización El Paraíso
Carretera de Cádiz km167
Estepona
Tel: 952-883-000
Fax: 952-882-019
www.hotelparaisocostadelsol.com
Located on a hilltop surrounded by golf courses, with wonderful views of the Mediterranean. Fitness centre. 175 rooms. €€€

Albero Lodge
Calle Tamesis 16
Finca La Cancelada
Estepona
Tel: 952-880-700
Fax: 952-885-238
www.alberolodge.com
Delightful, stylish nine-room hotel set in a converted villa not far from the beach, and surrounded by gardens. €€

Golf Hotel Guadalmina
Urbanización Guadalmina Baja
Marbella
Tel: 952-882-211
Fax: 952-882-291
www.hotelguadalmina.com
A tranquil location by the beach, surrounded by golf courses and gardens. Close to San Pedro and Puerto Banús. 177 rooms. €€

Diana Park
Carretera de Cádiz km168.5
Estepona
Tel: 952-887-659
Fax: 952-884-279
www.marbellainnhoteles.com
Pleasant, modern hotel set midway between Estepona and Marbella, with access to many sports facilities. Beach club. 90 rooms. €€

Hotel La Cartuja
Campos de la Cartuja
Carretera Benahavís km1.5
Tel: 952-882-270
Fax: 952-882-086
www.lacartuja.com
Stylish hotel overlooking the Atalaya golf course, just inland from the sea. A variety of suites and self-catering apartments, pools, sports facilities and a good restaurant. €€

East of Marbella
La Cala Resort
La Cala de Mijas
Mijas–Costa
Tel: 952-669-000
Fax: 952-669-039
www.lacala.com
The atmosphere at the stylish La Cala Resort is refreshingly relaxed. Not only is the hotel surrounded by golf courses, but its large rooms' picture windows overlook some of the fairways. 107 rooms. €€€

Don Carlos
Carretera de Cadiz km192
Marbella
Tel: 952-831-140/952-768-800
Fax: 952-833-429
www.hoteldoncarlos.com
Rising high above the pine woods, near the beach approximately 11km (7 miles) to the east of central Marbella, the Don Carlos hotel features a tennis club, beach club and the lively Oh! Marbella disco. 262 rooms. €€€

Left: Marbella Club Hotel

Guadalpin Byblos Andaluz
Urbanización Mijas-Golf
Mijas Costa, Málaga
Tel: 952-473-050
Fax: 952-476-783
www.byblos-andaluz.com
An Andalusian-style spa hotel, and the perfect choice for anyone who wants to pamper themselves in palatial splendour. It adjoins a golf course, and its health centre offers thalassotherapy treatments (based on sea water), massage and so forth. 144 rooms. €€€

Hotel Mijas
Urbanización Tamisa 2
Mijas
Tel: 952-485-800
Fax: 952-485-825
www.hotelmijas.es
This modern, airy hotel with lovely, ample gardens is on the periphery of the picture-postcard village of Mijas, and has some of the best views on the coast. 204 rooms. €€

Inland from Marbella
Castillo de Monda
El Castillo
Monda
Tel: 952-457-142
Fax: 952-457-336
www.mondacastle.com
On a hilltop overlooking the village of Monda, the Castillo de Monda incorporates the remains of the original fortress, and, in keeping with the location, is designed as a Moorish-style castle, with the interior décor following the theme. 23 rooms. €€

Refugio del Juanar
Sierra Blanca
Ojén
Tel: 952-881-000
Fax: 952-881-001
www.juanar.com
The Refugio del Juanar is a rustic mountain retreat in a former royal hunting lodge right in the middle of a forest in the mountains just inland from Marbella. The Marqués de Larios had the building constructed for his hunting parties. The hotel is now operated by a workers' co-operative. In season, the restaurant serves delicious game dishes. 26 rooms. €€

GETTING AROUND

By Car
The biggest international car hire firms are represented in Marbella and also at Málaga airport, but it may be cheaper to organise your transport before arriving in Spain. Some airlines have 'fly-drive' packages. You might find companies advertising budget car rentals in the travel pages of newspapers in your home country and you will certainly find some on the Internet. There are some 40 local firms and they generally offer better rates than the big international operators. Four local firms to try are:

ATA
Adva. Ricardo Soriano, Marbella
Tel: 952-828-637

Helle Hollis
Calle Camilo José Cela 21, Marbella
Tel: 952-823-038
Fax: 952-822-711

Niza Car Interrent Cars SL
Calle Camilo José Cela 40, Marbella.
Tel: 952-770-931
Fax: 952-771-352

Rual
Calle Luís Braille 22
San Pedro de Alcántara
Tel: 952-780-408
Fax: 952-786-890

Although the rules of the road are much the same as in the rest of Western Europe, Spain suffers from a much higher than average road accident and death rate. Eccentric (to say nothing of bad) driving is a hazard.

The N340/A7 dual carriageway is the main road along the coast and can get very busy around Málaga. Inland, the A7 motorway runs from Málaga to Estepona and beyond. This is a toll highway in three of its sections: one to Seville, one to Córdoba and one to Granada. If you overshoot your destination, look for a *Cambio de Sentido* sign, at which you can do a U-turn.

Car hire firms ought to notify you of the procedure in case of accident or breakdown. If you are in your own car, your travel or car-insurance company might issue special

practical information

instructions and organise the arrangements. You may need to get a *grua* (towing truck) and find a *taller de reparaciones* (repair shop). In many cases foreign motoring organisations have reciprocal arrangements with the Real Automóvil Club de España, calle Córdoba 17, Málaga (tel: 952-229-836).

Gasolineras (petrol/gas stations) sell super (97 octane), unleaded (*sin plomo* 96 and 98), and *gas oil* (diesel). Most stations are open 24 hours a day.

Drivers from EU countries, Switzerland and Norway bringing their own cars no longer need a Green Card for insurance purposes or an international driving licence – as already mentioned, a licence from your home country is sufficient whether you are driving your own car or hiring. If in doubt, check before leaving home

By Bus and Taxi

Marbella, Málaga and the larger resorts all have reasonably frequent and reliable bus services. The buses are comfortable and fares very reasonable.

Taxis are plentiful and relatively cheap in all urban centres. Agree on the fare in advance on longer trips. The rates are fixed on most journeys.

COMMUNICATIONS AND MEDIA

Keeping in Touch

Post offices *(Correos)* open Monday–Friday 9am– 2pm, also Saturday 9am–1pm at Jacinto Behavente 14, Marbella (tel: 952-772-898), and Calle Hernán Cortés, San Pedro de Alcántara (tel: 952-780-393).

To phone abroad, dial the international access code 00, then the country code:
Australia (61)
United Kingdom (44)
US and Canada (1)

Media

The Málaga daily newspaper *Sur* publishes a free English-language edition on Friday. *Absolute Marbella* is a colour glossy devoted to Marbella lifestyle. *Die Aktuelle* covers the Costa del Sol in German. *Solkysten* does the same for Scandinavians. Several radio stations broadcast in English, including the Marbella-based OCI (101.6 FM). Billboards and flyers also publicise special events.

HOURS AND HOLIDAYS

Business Hours

Most business are open Monday–Saturday 9 or 10am–1.30 or 2pm, then, following the *siesta* hours, 4 or 5pm–8 or 9pm. A number of shops close on Saturday afternoon; some supermarkets and department stores stay open later. On Sunday and public holidays, you should find a number of supermarkets and tourist shops plying their wares.

Public Holidays

In addition to local *fiestas* (June 11, Oct 19 in Marbella) and the changeable dates of the Easter holidays, public holidays in Andalucía are as follows:

1 January	Año Nuevo
6 January	Día de los Reyes
28 February	Día de Andalucía
1 May	Día del Trabajo
15 August	Asunción
12 October	Hispanidad (Columbus Day)
1 November	Todos los Santos (All Saints' Day)
6 December	Constitution Day
8 December	Inmaculada Concepción
25 December	Navidad (Christmas)

Right: forward planning

EMERGENCIES

Police

The *Policia Nacional* (tel: 091) deals with Spain's internal security and with law and order in the main urban areas. Its members are easily distinguishable by their navy blue uniforms. The HQ in Marbella is at Avenida Arias de Velasco, tel: 952-762-600. To report a crime you can call tel: 952-102-112.

The *Guardia Civil* (tel: 062) is responsible for law and order on the coast, in outlying towns and in rural areas. Its members wear green uniforms. Its HQ is at Plaza Leganitos in Marbella (tel: 952-770-344). It also runs the highway patrol from Marbella's Calle San Antonio (tel: 952-772-549).

The *Policia Local* (tel: 092), in blue but with checked bands, are mainly responsible for urban traffic control and civil protection. Its main police station is at Juan de la Cierva 3,Marbella (tel: 952-762-600).

Robbery

Thefts from cars or from private or hotel accommodation are not unknown, and mugging has also become a public hazard in the main cities. The need to feed a drug dependence is the motivation for many street crimes, especially in cities such as Málaga and Seville. Take sensible precautions, as you would anywhere, and be discreet with valuables such as wallets, cameras and jewellery. Be vigilant when getting money from ATMs. Don't leave valuables lying around your hotel room when you are not there.

Accident and Sickness

For residents of EU countries, the national health services provide a European Health Insurance Card (EHIC) to replace the old E111 form (www.ehic.org.uk). This enables you to benefit from reciprocal arrangements with SAS, Andalucía's public health service, which is generally excellent. However, to cover all eventualities, it is best to take out private health insurance.

The SAS Centro de Salud (Health Centre; tel: 952-772-184) is located on Plaza Leganitos, and the general hospital (Hospital Comarcal Costa del Sol, tel: 952-862-748) is just east of the town, opposite Hotel Los Monteros.

Marbella has a very large population of *medicos* (doctors) in all the specialised fields. There are also a number of private clinics from which you can obtain local advice and recommendations. The private UPS Hospital de Marbella (tel: 952-774-200) is at Avenida Severo Ochoa 22.

Pharmacies *(Farmacias)* are identified by green or red crosses and can often advise and deal directly with minor ailments. Outside normal shopping hours they display the name and address of the nearest *farmacia de guardia* which will be open.

Emergency Numbers

General Emergencies Tel: 112
National Police Tel: 091
Local Police Tel: 092
Medical Emergencies Tel: 061
Fire Brigade *(Bomberos)* Tel: 952-774-369

SPORT

Golf

There are several golf courses within the town boundaries of Marbella, and more within a short travelling distance. Non-members can have difficulty in getting a game during weekends and school holidays. One solution is to settle for inconvenient starting times, such as very early in the morning or in the midday sun on hot summer days.

Premier hotels have arrangements with particular courses but this doesn't necessarily help with booking a game at a convenient time. The best advice is to book a starting time well in advance through your hotel's concierge or direct with the club.

High demand means that green fees are relatively expensive – check them out in advance. In order to play a round, you will need to bring your handicap card from your home club.

All the clubs have professional coaches, and golf clubs and cart rentals for hire. The majority also rent out buggies. All have a bar and restaurant and most have a swimming pool and tennis courts. Málaga's provincial tourist board publishes relevant information, or see *Andalucía Golf* and *Sun Golf* – both of which are informative local publications.

Tennis
Most of Marbella's top hotels have excellent tennis facilities; hotel guests have court-rental priority. You have to be either a guest or a member to play at the top-notch **Puente Romano Tennis and Fitness Club** (tel: 952-820-900). Other hotels with good facilities include the Hotel Los Monteros (tel: 952-771-700), with 10 quick-surface courts, and the Hotel Don Carlos (tel: 952-768-800).

Tennis clubs include La Dama de Noche, the only illuminated course in Europe, in Camino del Ángel, Nueva Andalucía (tel: 952-818-150); and the Club de Tenis El Casco (tel: 952-837-651) in Urbanización El Rosario, east of Marbella.

Horse Riding
The country inland is ideal for horse trekking. Horse-riding centres include: Club Hípico Los Caireles, Hacienda Cortés, Finca El Almendral, Marbella (tel: 630-852-459); Hurricane Hotel, Tarifa, tel: 956-684-919; Centro Ecuestre Cañada Alta, Camino Almendrales, Málaga (tel: 952-268-943).

USEFUL INFORMATION

Tourist Offices in UK and US
79 New Cavendish Street, London W1W 6XB, tel: 0207 486 8077 (visits by prior appointment only); www.spain.info.
666 Fifth Avenue, New York, NY 10103, tel: 212-265 8822, fax: 212-265 8864; www.okspain.org.

Tourist Offices in Spain
Marbella: Plaza de los Naranjos, tel: 952-823-550; Glorieta de la Fontanilla, tel: 952-771-442. **San Pedro de Alcántara**: Avenida Marqués del Duero, tel: 952-785-252. **Málaga**, Avenida Cervantes, tel: 952-134-730; Pasaje de Chinitas, tel: 952-213-445. www.marbella.es.

Consulates (Consulados)
Many countries maintain local consulates, primarily in Málaga. Police, tourist offices and hotels can provide addresses and phone numbers. These include: Germany: 952-363-591; UK: 952-352-300; USA: 952-474-891; Canada: 952-223-346.

FURTHER READING

Travel Information
Insight Regional Guide: Southern Spain (Apa Publications). A detailed account of the region's history, culture and people with an emphasis on sights and activities for visitors, plus full-colour photography and maps.
Insight Pocket Guide: Southern Spain (Apa Publications). A concise introduction to both the wonders and the practical details of the area, complete with pull-out map.

Culture
Death in the Afternoon, by Ernest Hemingway (Cape). The American novelist's account of the bullfifght. Maligned by purists but an informative and gripping read.
In Search of the Firedance, by James Woodall (Sinclair Stevenson). Everything you need to know about flamenco and its origins.

Food and Wine
Cooking in Spain, by Janet Mendel (Santana). Encyclopaedic volume on Spanish cookery with 400 recipes and colourful insights into local cuisine.
Encyclopaedia of Spanish and Portuguese Wine, by Kathryn McWhirter and Charles Metcalfe (Simon & Schuster). A fine introduction to the new Iberian wines.

Right: fun in the sun and surf

credits

ACKNOWLEDGEMENTS

2/3, 51	**J. D Dallet**
1, 8/9, 21, 22T/B, 24, 33, 46, 52, 53T, 57 60B, 69, 71, 72	**Jerry Dennis**
10	**Andrew Eames**
16, 23, 25, 27T, 29, 30, 32B, 36, 37B, 40, 41T/B, 42, 45, 47, 50, 55, 58, 65, 83, 86	**Jens Poulsen**
15B	**Jan Read**
5, 6T/b, 7T/B, 15T, 20, 27b, 28, 31, 32T, 35T/B, 37T, 39T/b, 44, 49, 53B, 54, 56T/B, 59, 60T, 61, 63T/B, 66, 67, 68, 75, 77, 78, 79, 80, 84, 87, 89, 90	**Mark Read**
62	**Real Escuela Andaluza del Arte Ecuestre**
11, 64	**Bill Wassman**
Front cover	**Steve Allen/Photographer's Choice/Getty Images**
Original cartography	**Berndtson & Berndtson**

© APA Publications GmbH & Co. Verlag KG Singapore Branch, Singapore

Left: a festive *paseo* in full swing

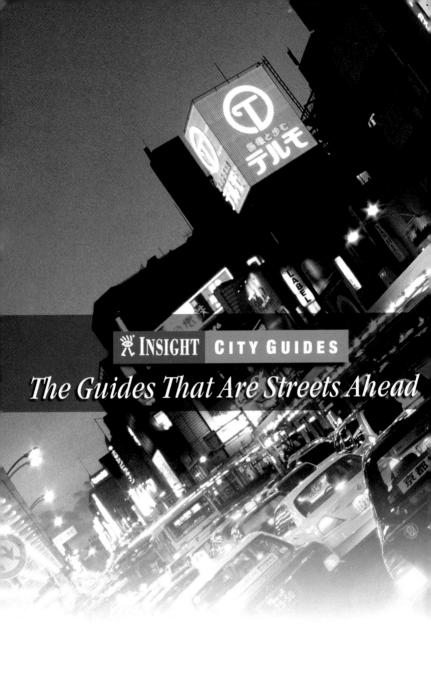

☆ INSIGHT | CITY GUIDES

The Guides That Are Streets Ahead

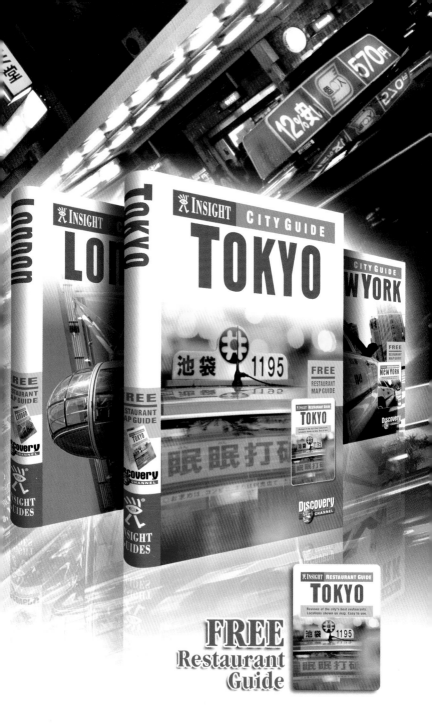

*Insight Guides to every major country
are also available*

www.insightguides.com

INDEX

Abd al-Rahman I 13
Abd al-Rahman III 13
accommodation
   see also individual itineraries
      and excursions
   listings 83–86
airports 81
Algeciras 36–37
Almansur 14
Almuñecar 67
Alora 49
Antequera 38–41, 67
   Alcazaba 39
   Arco de los Gigantes 38–39
   caves 38
   Convento del Carmen 40
   Convento de las Descalzas 40
   El Torcal de Antequera 41
   Iglesia de San Sebastián 40
   Iglesia de San Zoilo 40
   Iglesia de Santo Domingo 40
   Iglesia de la Madre de Dios 40
   Iglesia de los Remedios 40
   Museo Municipal 40
   Palacio del Marqués de las Escalonias 39
   Peña de Enamorados 39
   Real Colegiata de Santa María 39
   Torre del Papabellotas 39
Arcos de la Frontera 61
   Parador 64

Ardales 48–51

Balcón de Europa 64
bandits 16, 32–33
Benahavís 27
Benalmádena 51–53
business hours 87

Cabo de Trafalgar 58
Cádiz 62–64
   cathedral 64
   Museo de Cádiz 64
   Puerta de Tierra 63
   Torre Tavira 64
Carratraca 49
Casabermeja 49

Casares 45–46
   Baños Romanos 46
   castle 46
casinos 78
Castellar de la Frontera 46–48
Castillo Sohail 51
cinema 78
climate and seasons 81
Coín 48
Columbus, Christopher 15
Cómpeta 65
consulates 89
Cortes de la Frontera 37, 61
Costa Tropical 66–67
Cueva de la Pileta 61
Cuevas de Nerja 65
customs regulations 82

Dalí, Salvador 24
Drake, Sir Francis 63

Eating out 71, 72–76
   see also individual itineraries
      and excursions
El Bosque 60
el Bueno, Gúzman 57
El Chorro 48–51
   El Camino del Rey 51
   La Garganta 51
El Madroñal 32
El Torcal de Antequera 41
Embalse de la Concepción 42
Embalse de Guadarranque 47
emergencies 88
Estepona 44–45
   Plaza de los FLores 44
   Puerto de Estepona 45
   Torre del Reloj 44

Ferdinand of Aragon 15
festivals and events 79
food and drink 71, 72–76
flamenco 77
Franco, General 16
Frigiliana 64–66
Fuengirola 51
   zoo 51

Garganta de las Buitreroras 37
Gaucín 37, 46–48
  Castillo de Aguila 47
getting around 86–87
getting there 81–82
Gibraltar 54–55
  Apes' Den 55
  cable car 55
  Casamates Gate 54
  Gibraltar Museum 55
  Great Siege Tunnel 55
  St Michael's Cave 55
  Trafalgar Cemetery 55
  Upper Rock Nature Reserve 55
Granada 66, 67
Grazalema 59

Hakam II 14
Hemingway, Ernest 35
Hisham II 14
history and culture 11–17
Hollander, Gino 49
hotels 83–86

Infante, Blas 46
Isabella of Castile 15
Istán 42

Jardín de la Aguilas 52
Jerez de la Frontera 62–63
  Alcázar 62
  cathedral 62
  Puerto de Santa María 63
  Real Escuela Andaluza de Arte
    Ecuestre 63
Jimena de la Frontera 37
Jimera de Libar 37
Juan Carlos I 16

La Herradura 66
Laguna de la Fuente de Piedra 41
Los Arqueros Golf Course 32
La Axarquía 64–66
Los Caños de Meca 58
Los Lances 57
Los Reales 45

Málaga 15, 28–31
  Aduana 30

  Alcazaba 30
  Ayuntamiento (Town Hall) 30
  Café de Paris 30
  Casa del Consulado 29
  Casa Natal de Picasso 30
  Castillo de Gibralfaro 31
  Catedral 29
  Centro de Arte Contemporaneo 28
  Fuente Genovesa 30
  Iglesia del Sagrario 29
  Iglesia del Santo Cristo de la Salud
    29
  La Concepción botanical garden
    31, 41
  La Malagueta 30
  Museo Catredralicio 29
  Museo de Artes y Tradiciones
    Populares 28–29
  Museo Picasso 29
  Palacio Episcopal 29
  Parador 31
  Paseo del Parque 30
  Plaza de Toros 30
  Puerta de Atarazanas 28
  Restaurante Chinitas 30
  Teatro Romano 12, 30
Manilva 46
Marbella 16, 23–27
  Ayuntamiento 23
  Casa del Corregidor (Chief Magistrate's
    House) 23
  Ermita de Santiago 23
  Iglesia de Nuestra Señora de la
    Encarnación 23
  Marbella Club 16, 25
  Mezquita del Rey Abdulaziz 26
  Museo del Bonsai 23
  Museo del Grabado Contemporáneo 23
  Museo Ralli 26
  Paseo de la Alameda 24
  Plaza de los Naranjos 22
  Puente Romano 25
  Puerto Banús 25, 26–27
markets 69–70
media 87
Mijas 51–53
  Estupa de la Iluminación 52
  Museo Carromato de Max 52
  Plaza de Toros 52

Monda 48
money matters 82
Montenmedio Country Club 58
Museo Hollander 49
Museo de Pizarra 49

Nerja 21, 64–66
   Balcón de Europa 64
   Cuevas de Nerja 65
nightlife 77–78

Ojén 43
Ordoñez, Antonio 35

Parque de Ardales 49
Parque de la Paloma 53
Parque Natural de los Alcornocales
   37, 62
Parque Natural Sierra de las Nieves 32
Picasso, Pablo 21, 29, 30
Pizarra 49
police 88
postal services 87
public holidays 87
Pueblos Blancos (**White Towns**) 59–61
Puerto Banús 25, 26–27
Puerto de Estepona 45
Puerto de Sotogrande 48
Puerto Duquesa 46

Refugio de Juanar 43
restaurants 72–76
Ronda 32–37, 59
   Alameda del Tajo 35
   Alcázar 34
   Baños Arabes 34
   Casa del Gigante 34
   Casa del Rey Moro 33
   Camino de los Molinos 35
   Minarete de San Sebastián 34
   Museo del Bandolero 33
   Palacio del Marqués de Salvatierra 34
   Palacio de Mondragón 34
   Parador 32
   Plaza de Toros 34–35
   Puente Arabe 34, 37
   Puente Nuevo 33, 35
   Puente Viejo 34
   Puerta de Felipe V 34

   Tajo 32, 33, 35
Ronda la Vieja 12, 59
Ruinas de Bobastro 51

Salobreña 67
   Museo Histórico 67
   sugar mill 67
San Pablo de Buceite 37
San Roque 36
Sea Life Aquarium (Mijas) 52
Selwo Marina 53
Selwo Wildlife Park 44
Setenil 59
shopping 69–71
Sotogrande 46–48
sports 88–89
   golf 88
   horse-riding 89
   tennis 89
   windsurfing 56
Strait of Gibraltar 55

Tapas 72–73
Tarifa 56–58
   Baelo Claudia 57–58
   Castillo de Guzmán 57
   Los Lances 57
   watersports 56
Teleférico (Benalmádena) 52
telephones 87
time differences 81
Tivoli World 52
Torremolinos 51–53
   Cuesta del Tajo 53
   Molino de Rosario 53
   Playa de Carihuela 53
Torrox 65
tourist offices 89
transport 81–82, 86–87

Ubrique 60

Vejer de la Frontera 58
Venta Los Reales 45
von Hohenlohe, Alfonso 16

Welles, Orson 35

Zahara de la Sierra 61

Register with
HotelClub.com
and get £10!

At *HotelClub.com*, we reward our Members with discounts and free stays in their favourite hotels. As a Member, every booking made by you through *HotelClub.com* will earn you Member Dollars.

When you register, we will credit your account with **£10** which you can use for your next booking! The equivalent of **£10** will be credited in US$ to your Member account (as *HotelClub Member Dollars*). All you need to do is log on to *www.HotelClub.com/pocketguides*. Complete your details, including the Membership Number and Password located on the back of the *HotelClub.com* card.

Over 2.2 million Members already use Member Dollars to pay for all or part of their hotel bookings. Join now and start spending Member Dollars whenever and wherever you want – you are not restricted to specific hotels or dates!

With great savings of up to 60% on over 20,000 hotels across 97 countries, you are sure to find the perfect location for business or pleasure. Happy travels from *HotelClub.com!*